From Your Friends At **The MAILBOX**

DECEMBER

A MONTH OF REPRODUCIBLES AT YOUR FINGERTIPS!

Grades 2–3

Project Editor:
Amy Erickson

Editor:
Darcy Brown

Writers:
Darcy Brown, Rebecca Brudwick, Amy Erickson,
Heather Godwin, Todd Helms,
Cynthia Holcomb, Nicole Iacovazzi

Art Coordinator:
Clevell Harris

Artists:
Jennifer Tipton Bennett, Teresa Davidson,
Nick Greenwood, Clevell Harris, Susan Hodnett,
Sheila Krill, Rob Mayworth, Kimberly Richard

Cover Artist:
Jennifer Tipton Bennett

©1999 by THE EDUCATION CENTER, INC.
All rights reserved.
ISBN #1-56234-279-7

Manufactured in the United States

10 9 8 7 6 5 4 3 2 1

Table Of Contents

December Calendar 3
Daily activities for free-time fun.

Events And Activities For The Family 4
Three events and activities for parents and students to explore at home.

Oh, Boy! Gingerbread! 5
Packed with fresh ideas and reproducibles, this gingerbread unit is simply irresistible!

Hanukkah 11
Explore Hanukkah traditions with these creative projects and reproducibles.

Christmas 17
These holiday ideas and literature selections are perfect for welcoming the Christmas season.

Kwanzaa 23
Teach students about Kwanzaa with this bountiful harvest of fun-filled activities.

Jan Brett 29
Jan Brett's picture books and these related ideas are sure to delight your students.

Soaring Through The Solar System 33
Take students on a wonderful learning adventure with a unit that's out of this world!

Take Time For Teddy Bears! 41
Capture youngsters' interest with these skill-based teddy bear activities and reproducibles.

Warm Up To Winter! 47
The forecast calls for a blizzard of learning fun!

Mittens, Mittens, Mittens! 55
This "hand-y" unit is perfect for wintertime skill reinforcement.

Poinsettia Day 59
Student learning will grow and grow with these poinsettia-related ideas!

Answer Keys 63

December Free Time

Monday	Tuesday	Wednesday	Thursday	Friday
The first week of December is Cookie Cutter Week. Draw an unusual cookie cutter. Write about the cookies you would like to make with it.	December is International Calendar Awareness Month. Write about your favorite day of the week. Be sure to explain why you like it.	If each student wears two mittens, how many mittens do 15 students need? Solve this problem on another sheet of paper.	List as many words as you can that begin with *D*.	Chester Greenwood, the inventor of the earmuff, is honored on December 4. Do you prefer to wear a hat or earmuffs? Explain your answer on another sheet of paper.
Walt Disney was born on December 5, 1901. Draw a picture of the Disney® character you like the most. Then write about why it's your favorite.	If you could give your family any one gift, what would you give and why? Write your answer on another sheet of paper.	List the letters in *December* in a column. For each letter, write a word that describes December. **D**ecorations **E**lves **C**hristmas **E**ggnog **M**istletoe **B**rrrrrr **E**xciting **R**eindeer	One of America's greatest poets, Emily Dickinson, was born on December 10, 1830. Read one of her poems. Then draw a picture to illustrate it.	December brings the first snowstorms to many places. What would happen if there were a blizzard in July? Write and illustrate a story about a summer snowstorm.
Snowball and *gingerbread* are compound words. List at least ten other compound words. snowball gingerbread popcorn	How many boys and girls are in your class? Make a bar graph to show your answer. Remember to label your work.	December 15 is One Day. This day honors December celebrations including Christmas, Hanukkah, and Kwanzaa. Design and color a poster for this day.	Imagine that you are a snowperson. Write a story about your day.	The first crossword puzzle was created on December 21, 1913, by Arthur Wynne. Make a crossword puzzle and ask a friend to solve it.
Winter begins on December 21 or 22. Write a story about the things you like to do in winter. Then draw a picture to go with your story.	If there are 30 legs, how many reindeer and elves could there be? Write and illustrate two different answers.	Draw and color a new gift wrap pattern. Remember, a pattern repeats.	Write a list of 15 winter words. Beside each word, write the number of syllables it has.	Who is your hero? Is it a sports star, an actor, or someone else? Write about your hero.

Note To The Teacher: Have each student staple a copy of this page inside a file folder. Instruct students to store their completed work in their folders.

December
Events And Activities For The Family

Directions: Select at least one activity below to complete as a family by the end of December.
(Challenge: See if your family can complete all three activities.)

Gifts Of The Heart

Share the warmth of the holiday season with a family volunteer project. Discuss the ways your family can share the joy of giving, such as making cards for senior citizens, singing Christmas carols at a nursing home, or helping a neighbor in need. Then select one or more of these activities to do together. No doubt you'll want to make this rewarding experience a new family tradition!

Great Gift Idea

Help your family members make these unique scented soaps. They make "scent-sational" gifts for the holidays or for any time of the year!

Scented Soap Balls
(Makes five soap balls)

You need:
4 cups Ivory Snow® soap flakes
1/2 cup water
8–10 drops red or green food coloring
1 teaspoon peppermint extract
decorative fabric
ribbon

Directions:
1. Mix the water, food coloring, and extract in a large bowl.
2. Mix in the soap flakes (the mixture will be crumbly).
3. Shape the mixture into five balls, packing each ball firmly.
4. Allow the soap balls to dry overnight.
5. Wrap each ball with an eight-inch square of decorative fabric and tie it with a ribbon.

Take 12

Recognize the 12th month of the year with this timely tribute to 12! In the center of a large sheet of paper, write the numeral 12 with a colorful marker or a crayon. Then ask each family member to write a different way to make 12 using addition, subtraction, multiplication, or division. Display the paper in an easily accessible location, such as on your refrigerator door. Then, each day for a desired number of days, review the problems listed and challenge each family member to add a new way to make 12. Count on this math activity to result in dozens of creative solutions!

Note To The Teacher: Give one copy of this reproducible to each student at the beginning of the month. Encourage each family to complete at least one activity by the end of December.

Feature these tempting gingerbread ideas on your classroom menu of holiday activities!

Gingerbread Greetings

Looking for a sweet handmade card idea? Then try these gingerbread-house greetings with your youngsters! Give each student a brown construction-paper copy of the house pattern on page 6. Have him cut out his pattern and glue it onto a folded sheet of white construction paper as shown in figure 1. Next instruct him to cut out a white construction-paper copy of each house piece on page 6. Ask him to color the pieces as desired, cut them out, and glue them onto his house. Then have him carefully cut around his card through both layers of paper (see figure 2). To complete his card, he writes a holiday message or a seasonal poem inside the card, then signs it. Encourage each student to hand-deliver his special card to a loved one.

figure 1

figure 2

Spicy Ornaments

These cinnamon-scented ornaments are sure to spice up students' holidays! Give each youngster a six-inch tagboard cutout that is shaped like a ginger-bread man. Have him place his cutout on a slightly larger piece of waxed paper. Then instruct the youngster to paint a thin layer of glue on his cutout. Have him sprinkle ground cinnamon onto the glue and shake off the excess. Allow the glue to dry; then ask each student to decorate his ornament with a variety of craft supplies, such as sequins, black beads, and minirickrack. Finally, have each youngster loop a six-inch length of gold thread and tape it to the back of his ornament for a hanger (see the illustration).

Adventures In Gingerland

Here's a gem of a fairy-tale idea! In advance, copy each writing topic shown onto a different gingerbread-boy cutout and display it in a prominent classroom location. Then read with students your favorite version of "The Gingerbread Boy" and discuss the characters in the story. Next challenge each youngster to create her own gingerbread characters for a new fairy tale. Give each youngster a copy of page 7. Have the student write on her sheet a story that is based on one of the displayed topics and features her characters. Invite each youngster to share her completed story. Then staple the stories to a bulletin board titled "Adventures In Gingerland."

Goldilocks And The Three Gingerbread Men

Little Red Riding Hood And The Gingerbread Family

The Fairy Godmother Meets The Gingerbread Characters

Snow White And The Seven Gingerbread Boys

House Pattern

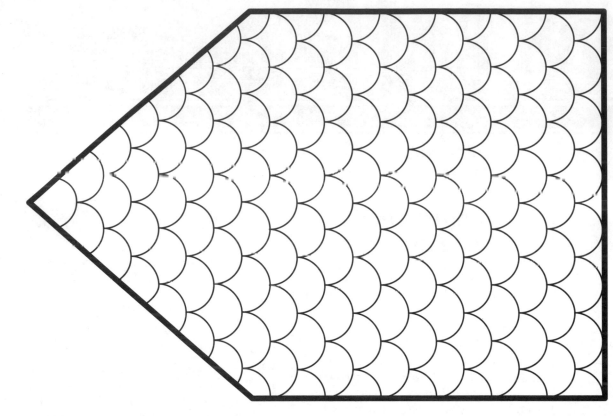

House Pieces

Note To The Teacher: Use with "Gingerbread Greetings" on page 5.

_____

_____

_____

_____

_____

_____

_____

_____

_____

_____

_____

_____

_____

_____

Note To The Teacher: Use with "Adventures In Gingerland" on page 5.

Name _____

Home, Sweet Gingerbread Home

Cut out the rod and blocks on the bold lines.
Snip apart the ones blocks on the dotted lines.
Use the rod and blocks to measure each side of the house.
Write the number of tens and ones in the matching box.

A

1. Side A to B

tens	ones

4. Side C to E

tens	ones

B   **C**

2. Side B to D

tens	ones

5. Side A to C

tens	ones

3. Side D to E

tens	ones

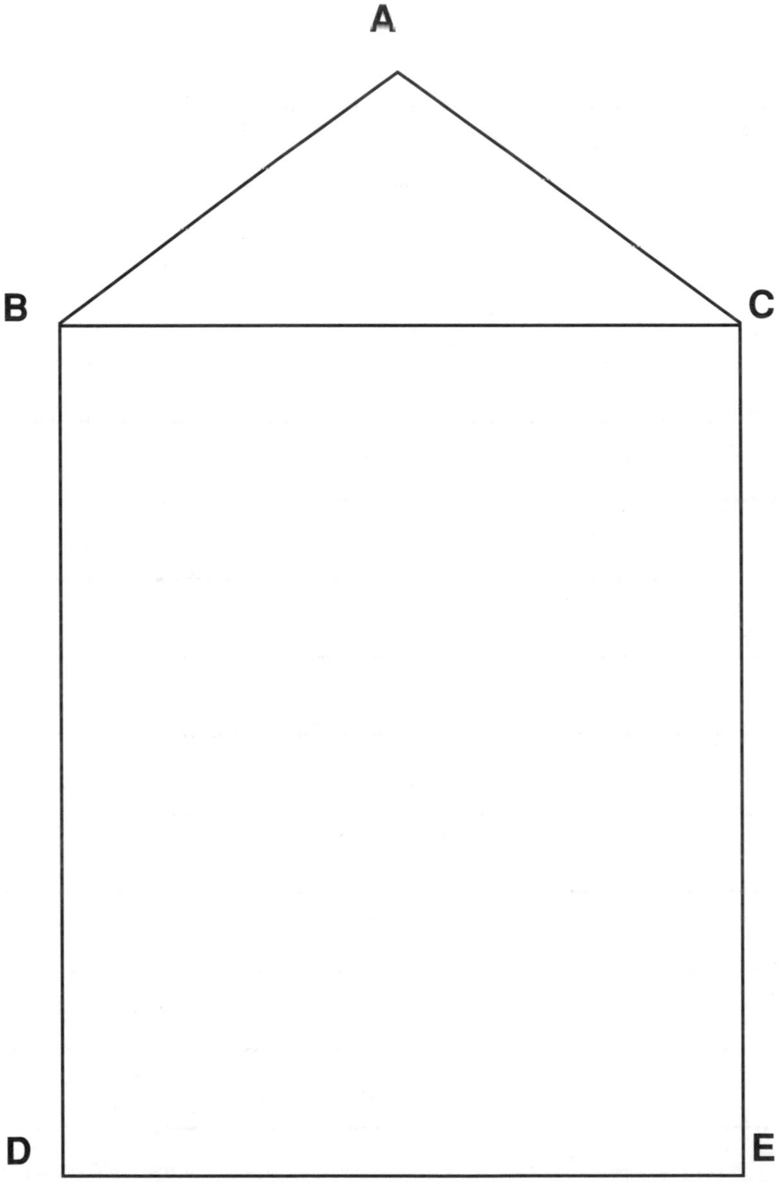

6. Side B to C

tens	ones

D   **E**

Bonus Box: How many blocks does the **outside** edge of the house measure? Add together the length of each outside edge to find the answer. Then write your answer in the blank. _____

©1999 The Education Center, Inc. • *December Monthly Reproducibles* • Grades 2–3 • TEC969 • Key p. 63

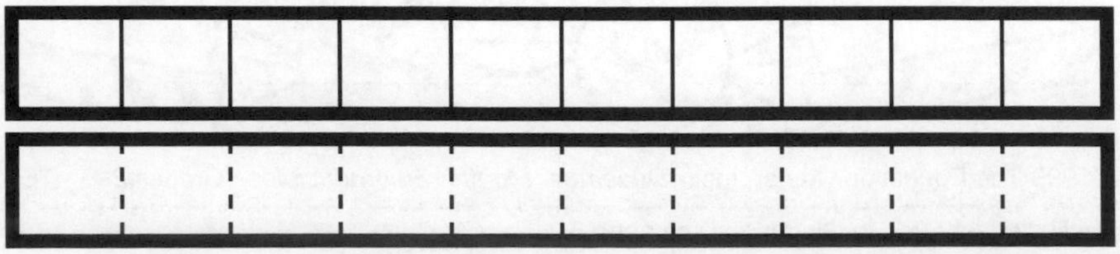

tens rod

ones blocks

Gingerbread Fashions

These gingerbread boys and girls are wearing the latest fashions!
Read each word.
Use pairs of words to make compound words. (Use each word only once.)
Write the compound words on the lines.
Then color the matching outfits.

Bonus Box:
On the back of this sheet, write a story using the compound words.

_____   _____   _____

_____   _____   _____

Name _____

Ginger All The Way

Help Miss Spice find the way to her house.
Start with *too* and follow the path.
Color each gumdrop that rhymes with *chew*.

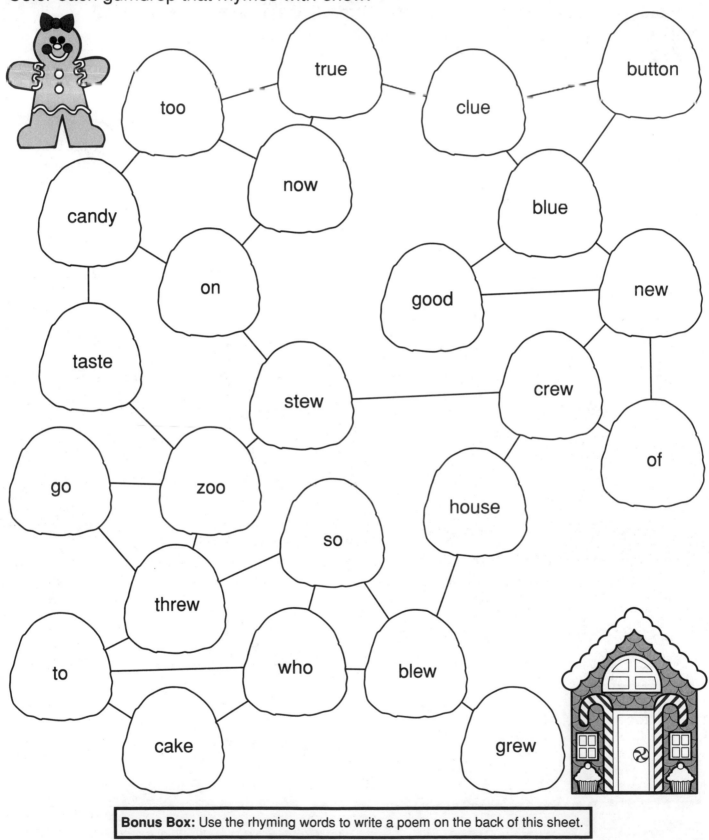

Bonus Box: Use the rhyming words to write a poem on the back of this sheet.

©1999 The Education Center, Inc. • *December Monthly Reproducibles* • Grades 2–3 • TEC969 • Key p. 63

HANUKKAH

Brighten your classroom with these fun-filled ideas for Hanukkah, the Feast Of Lights.

The Lights Of Hanukkah

Hanukkah is an eight-day celebration that commemorates the Jews' victory over Syrian invaders more than 2,000 years ago. According to legend, when the Jews reclaimed their temple, a lamp inside the building burned for eight nights even though it held only a small amount of oil. To remember this miraculous event, observers of Hanukkah use a *menorah,* a special candelabrum that holds nine candles. The center candle, or *shammash,* is used to light the other candles. One candle is lit on the first night of Hanukkah and an additional candle is lit on each of the remaining nights of this celebration.

Share this information with students, then have each youngster make a decorative menorah. Give each student a white tagboard copy of page 12. Have him personalize, color, and cut out the pattern. Next instruct the youngster to firmly crease the dotted lines so that the candles stand as shown. Then have each student cut two flames from yellow construction paper. Ask him to glue the first flame to the shammash and the second flame to the far left candle. Then display students' projects on an easily accessible windowsill or shelf. On each of the following days, have each student add a flame, from left to right, to one of his remaining candles until his entire menorah is "lit."

Star Of David Mobiles

No Hanukkah unit would be complete without the Star of David, the symbol of Judaism. Feature this special star with these shimmering mobiles. Give each student 18 flat toothpicks, a six-inch square of waxed paper, glitter, thread, and glue. Instruct the student to place the waxed paper on her desk for a workmat. To begin, she puts a drop of glue on each end of three toothpicks. Then she joins the toothpicks together to form a triangle. The student repeats the process with her remaining toothpicks, then sets aside the triangles to dry. Next the youngster glues one of her triangles atop another as shown to create a Star of David. She repeats this step with her remaining triangles to make three stars. Next the student applies a thin layer of glue atop each triangle, then sprinkles glitter onto the glue. After her project has dried completely, help the student tie her stars together with thread (see the illustration). Then suspend each student's mobile from the ceiling with string to make a dazzling holiday display!

Special Symbols

Set student learning aglow with this Hanukkah vocabulary booklet! Give each student a copy of page 13. Have him color and cut out each symbol as you explain its significance using the information below. Next ask him to glue each cutout near the top of a separate sheet of paper and write about the symbol below its picture. Instruct him to staple his pages between two construction-paper covers, then personalize and title the resulting booklet.

- A **dreidel** is a four-sided top with a Hebrew letter on each side. It's used to play a popular game during Hanukkah.
- **Gelt** is money—usually coins—that is given to children during Hanukkah. Sometimes chocolate coins wrapped in gold foil are used as gelt for the dreidel game.
- **Latkes** are potato pancakes fried in oil. They are a special Hanukkah treat.
- A **menorah** is a special holder for Hanukkah candles. The center candle, or *shammash,* is used to light the other eight candles.
- The **Star of David** is the symbol of Judaism.

Menorah
Use with "The Lights Of Hanukkah" on page 11.

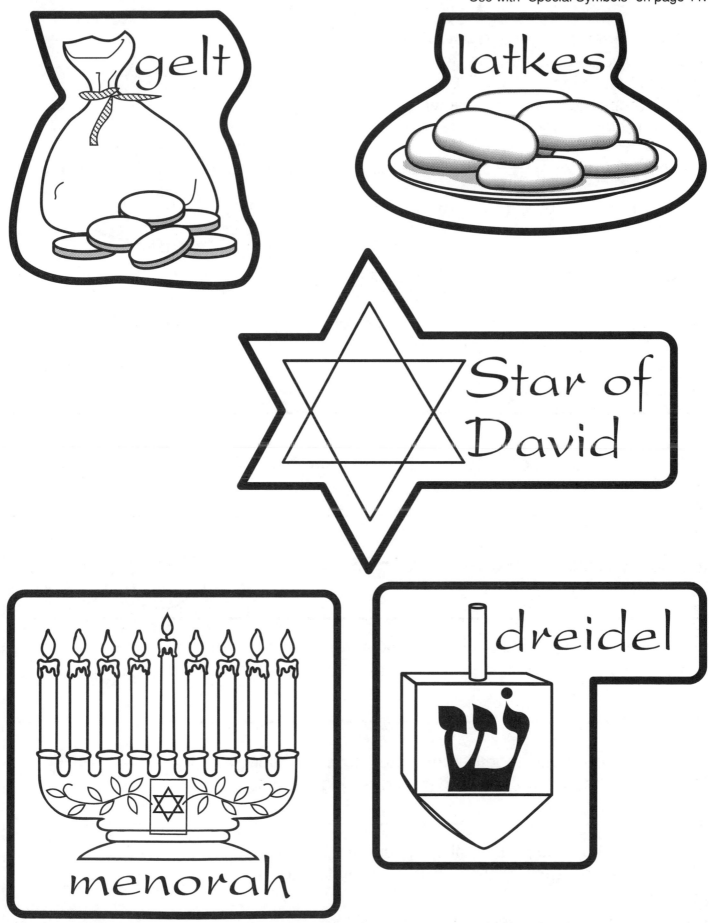

Name _____

Let's Make Latkes!

Cut out the recipe card and directions.
Glue the recipe card near the top of a sheet of paper.
Read the directions.
Glue the directions in order below the recipe card.
Try the recipe at home!

Hanukkah Latkes
(Makes 24 small latkes)

4 large potatoes, peeled and grated
1/4 onion, chopped
2 eggs
1/4 cup flour
1 teaspoon salt
1/4 teaspoon pepper
1/4 teaspoon baking powder
oil

©1999 The Education Center, Inc. • *December Monthly Reproducibles* • Grades 2–3 • TEC969 • Key p. 63

Fry both sides of the latkes until they are browned.

Before you start to cook, ask a grown-up to help you.

Use a spatula to take the cooked latkes from the skillet. Place the latkes on paper towels to cool; then serve them.

In a large bowl, mix together the potatoes, onion, and eggs. Add the flour, salt, pepper, and baking powder.

Carefully drop spoonfuls of the mixture into a skillet of hot oil. Flatten each spoonful with a spoon to make latkes.

Note To The Teacher: To complete this sheet, each student will need glue, scissors, and a blank sheet of paper.

Name _____

It's Hanukkah Time!

There is so much to do during Hanukkah!
Read each numbered sentence.
Find the matching clock and trace its hands.
Then write the letter of the clock in the blank.

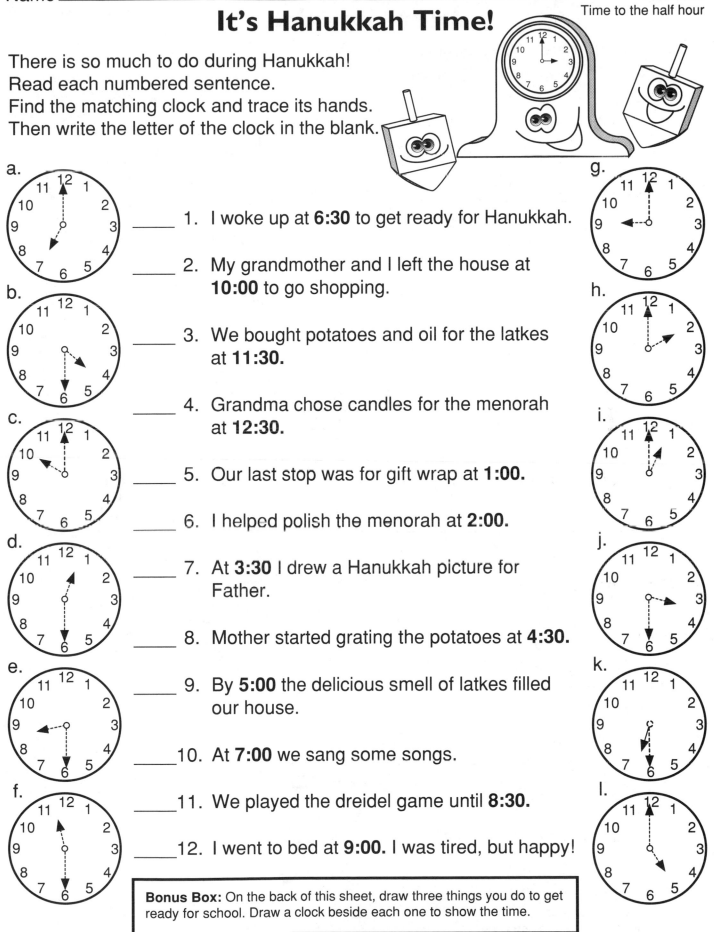

a.

b.

c.

d.

e.

f.

g.

h.

i.

j.

k.

l.

_____ 1. I woke up at **6:30** to get ready for Hanukkah.

_____ 2. My grandmother and I left the house at **10:00** to go shopping.

_____ 3. We bought potatoes and oil for the latkes at **11:30**.

_____ 4. Grandma chose candles for the menorah at **12:30**.

_____ 5. Our last stop was for gift wrap at **1:00**.

_____ 6. I helped polish the menorah at **2:00**.

_____ 7. At **3:30** I drew a Hanukkah picture for Father.

_____ 8. Mother started grating the potatoes at **4:30**.

_____ 9. By **5:00** the delicious smell of latkes filled our house.

_____ 10. At **7:00** we sang some songs.

_____ 11. We played the dreidel game until **8:30**.

_____ 12. I went to bed at **9:00**. I was tired, but happy!

Bonus Box: On the back of this sheet, draw three things you do to get ready for school. Draw a clock beside each one to show the time.

Name _____

Dizzy Dreidels

Hanukkah
Greater/less than to 1,000

Write a numeral from 1 to 999 on each blank.
Make sure the number sentence is true.

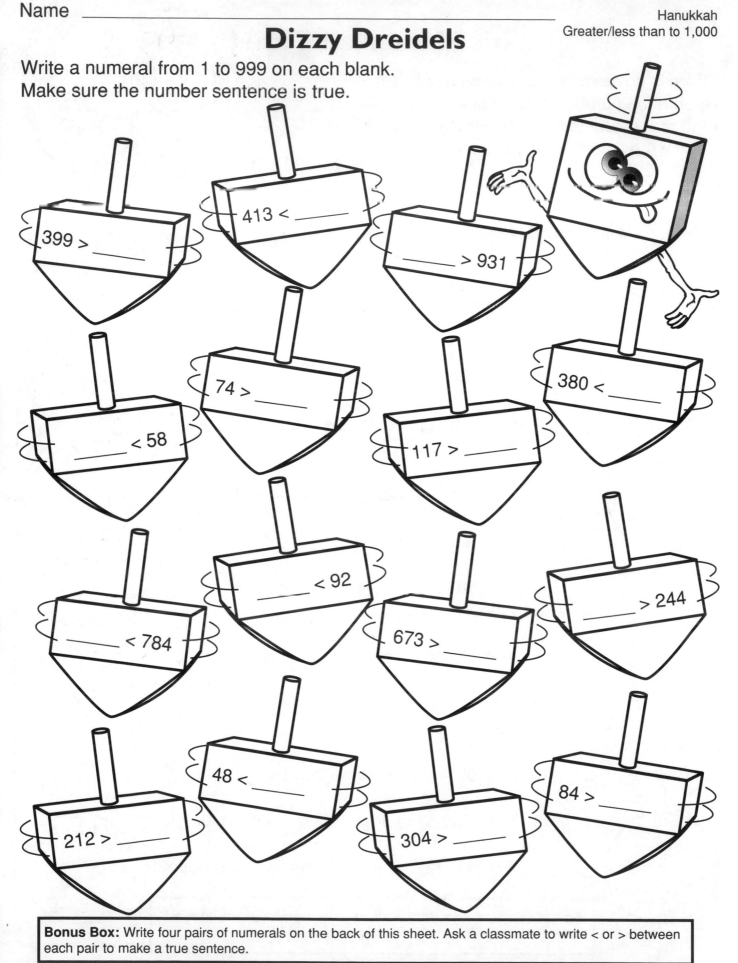

399 > _____

413 < _____

_____ > 931

74 > _____

_____ < 58

117 > _____

380 < _____

_____ < 784

_____ < 92

673 > _____

_____ > 244

212 > _____

48 < _____

304 > _____

84 > _____

Bonus Box: Write four pairs of numerals on the back of this sheet. Ask a classmate to write < or > between each pair to make a true sentence.

Christmas

Trim the holiday season with these Christmas ideas and literature selections!

Handmade Ornaments

Bring the excitement of creating handmade ornaments into the classroom with this simple project! Tell students that the tradition of decorating Christmas trees began many years ago. In the early 1600s, German Christmas trees were trimmed with decorations such as fruits, nuts, gingerbread, and paper flowers. Fruits and handmade ornaments decorated the Christmas trees in many early American homes, too. Later, colored glass ornaments replaced the fruits, and people began decorating their trees with store-bought ornaments.

Have each student make his own handmade decoration. To make a wreath ornament, each student needs a 4-inch tagboard circle with a 1 3/4-inch hole in the center and a piece of waxed paper for a workmat. He also needs two tablespoons dried peas, one tablespoon dried red beans, red ribbon, string, a plastic spoon, and a paper cup. Make a solution of two parts glue and one part water. Then have each student mix in his cup the peas and beans with 1 1/2 tablespoons of the glue solution until they are well coated. Ask him to evenly spoon the mixture onto his circle. Set aside the project to dry overnight. Then have each student make a ribbon bow and glue it onto his ornament as shown. Instruct him to thread a length of string through the center of his decoration and tie the ends together for a hanger. Encourage each student to take his completed ornament home for a special decoration or gift.

"Tree-rific" Trimmers

Reinforce math skills with this "tree-rific" center! To prepare the center, cut from a large piece of green bulletin-board paper a Christmas tree that is approximately three feet tall; then laminate the cutout for durability. Make four colored construction-paper copies of page 18. Cut out and number each ornament. Program the front of each ornament with a math problem and the back of the ornament with the answer. Program the answer sheet (page 19) with directions for solving the problems on the ornaments; then duplicate a class supply. Display the tree in an easily accessible place at a center. Tape the ornaments onto the tree and place the prepared answer sheets nearby. To use the center, a student selects an ornament and solves its problem on her answer sheet. She continues in a like manner until she has solved all of the problems. Then the youngster removes the ornaments and checks her work. She places the ornaments back on the tree to prepare the center for the next student.

Ornament problems on the tree:

1. $13 + 25$
2. $88 - 19$
3. $73 + 27$
4. $58 + 19$
5. $76 - 34$
6. $29 + 31$
7. $43 - 9$
8. $16 + 15$

Sensational Seasonal Selections

A Pussycat's Christmas by Margaret Wise Brown (HarperCollins Children's Books, 1994)

Christmas On An Island by Gail Gibbons (Morrow Junior Books, 1994)

The Christmas Blizzard by Helen Ketteman (Scholastic Inc., 1995)

Santa's Book Of Names by David McPhail (Little, Brown And Company; 1997)

The Christmas Miracle Of Jonathan Toomey by Susan Wojciechowski (Candlewick Press, 1995)

17

Ornament Patterns

Use with " 'Tree-rific' Trimmers" on page 17.

"Tree-rific" Trimmers

Directions:

Note To The Teacher: Use with " 'Tree-rific' Trimmers" on page 17.

19

Stocking Stuffers

Count the coins in each box.
Write the total on the top part of the stocking.
If the stocking has an **even** total, color the rest of it **red**.
If the stocking has an **odd** total, color the rest of it **green**.

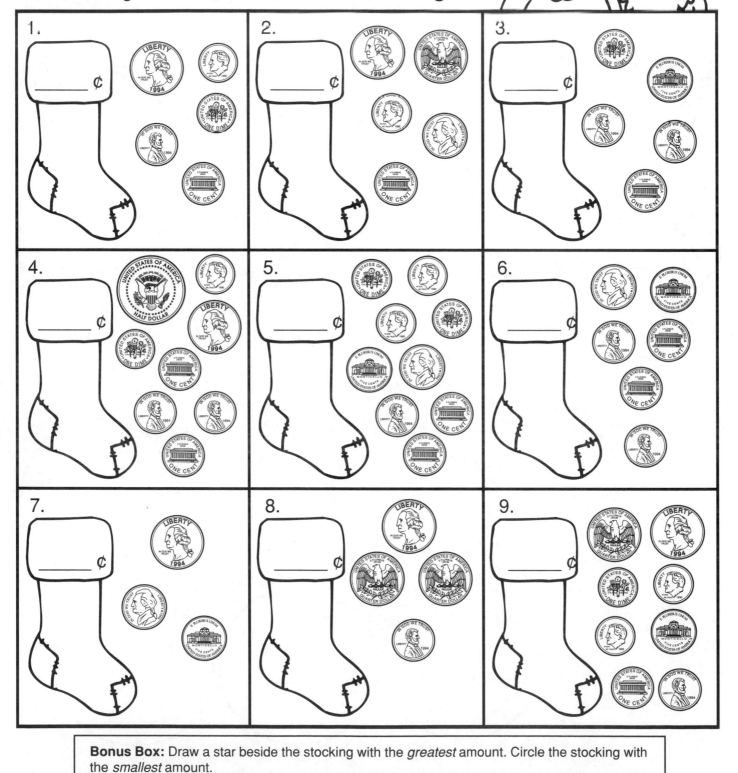

Bonus Box: Draw a star beside the stocking with the *greatest* amount. Circle the stocking with the *smallest* amount.

©1999 The Education Center, Inc. • *December Monthly Reproducibles* • Grades 2–3 • TEC969 • Key p. 63

Santa's Hurried Helpers

Santa's elves have had a busy week!
Read each sentence.
Circle the letters that need to be capitalized.

Hint: Look at the hat beside each sentence. It shows how many letters to circle.

NORTH POLE

3 1. on monday the elves helped santa read his letters.

3 2. on tuesday they decided what toys to make for christmas presents.

3 3. wednesday morning was a very busy time at the north pole.

2 4. the elves were working hard to build toy trains for santa's sack.

2 5. then an elf named eddie spilled a can of red paint.

3 6. his friends ellen and ernie helped him clean it up.

4 7. on thursday the elves helped mrs. claus make dolls.

3 8. all day friday, the elves wrapped candy for christmas stockings.

3 9. by saturday the elves were dreaming of vacations in hawaii.

2 10. they all agreed that december is the busiest month of the year!

Bonus Box: On the back of this sheet, write about a Christmas when you were very busy. Remember to use capital letters.

Name _____

Santa's Sack

Help Santa fill his sack!
Cut out the pictures.
Glue them in ABC order on Santa's sack.

1.	2.	3.	4.	5.	6.
7.	8.	9.	10.	11.	12.

Bonus Box: What else could Santa have in his sack? On the back of this sheet, draw and color six more things. Then list their names in ABC order.

©1999 The Education Center, Inc. • *December Monthly Reproducibles* • Grades 2–3 • TEC969 • Key p. 63

| drum | baseball | puppy | skates | teddy bear | boat |
| train | doll | mittens | marbles | game | sled |

Kwanzaa

Kwanzaa, the celebration of traditional African-American values, originated in 1966. This seven-day event begins on December 26, the time of the African harvest, and focuses on a different guiding principle each day.

First Fruits

What better way to recognize Kwanzaa, a harvesttime holiday, than by sampling some delicious fruits? Explain to students that *Kwanzaa* means the "first fruits of the harvest." Then invite each youngster to sample several fresh fruits. (See the illustration for suggestions. Also be sure to check with parents about food allergies.) After each student has tasted the fruit, enlist his help to create a related class graph. Label a sheet of chart paper with each of the food choices. Then give a simple fruit-shaped cutout to each youngster. Have him write his name in the middle of the cutout, then glue it in the column of the food he likes best. Discuss the resulting graph with youngsters. Follow up this activity by having each student make a Venn diagram that shows the similarities and differences of two foods he sampled.

Fruits From Africa

bananas
cashews
kiwis
lemons
limes
papayas
pineapple
oranges

The Principles Of Kwanzaa

Introduce the seven principles of Kwanzaa with this group poster project! In advance, cut seven one-yard lengths of white bulletin-board paper. Across the top of each paper write a different Kwanzaa principle (refer to the list on page 24). Give each youngster a copy of the principles; then read and discuss the meaning of each one. Divide students into seven groups and give each group a labeled poster. Instruct each group to decorate the poster to illustrate its principle. If desired, have each group make a vegetable-print border on its poster with red, green, and black paint (the colors of this holiday). Display the completed posters throughout your study of this holiday for a handy Kwanzaa reference.

Seven Celebration Symbols

Teach youngsters about important Kwanzaa symbols with these eye-catching mobiles! Give each student a white construction-paper copy of the patterns on pages 24 and 25. Discuss the name and meaning of each symbol. Have each youngster color and cut out her patterns, then pair each symbol card with the matching description card. Instruct her to tape a nine-inch length of yarn to the back of each pair of cards. Next ask her to decorate a 3" x 20" strip of tagboard as desired and tape each length of yarn to the back of her tagboard strip at even intervals. Help the youngster carefully bend her tagboard strip into a circle until the ends meet, then staple the ends together. To complete her project, have each student hole-punch the tagboard four times as shown. Then thread and knot a length of yarn at each hole and tie the yarn ends together. Suspend these mobiles from the ceiling to create a "class-y" Kwanzaa display.

Umoja
Unity—We help each other.

KWANZAA

Kwanzaa Principles

The Seven Principles Of Kwanzaa

1. **Umoja** (oo-MO-jah)
Unity—We help each other.

2. **Kujichagulia** (koo-jee-cha-goo-LEE-ah)
Self-determination—We decide things for ourselves.

3. **Ujima** (oo-JEE-mah)
Collective work and responsibility—We work together to make life better.

4. **Ujamaa** (oo-jah-MAH)
Cooperative economics—We support our community.

5. **Nia** (NEE-ah)
Purpose—We have a reason for living.

6. **Kuumba** (koo-OOM-bah)
Creativity—We use our hands and minds to make things.

7. **Imani** (ee-MAH-nee)
Faith—We believe in ourselves, our ancestors, and our future.

©1999 The Education Center, Inc.

Mobile Patterns

The **mkeka** (mm-KEH-kah) is a straw placemat. It is a symbol of African traditions.	**Mazao** (mah-ZAH-oh) are fruits and vegetables. They represent the hard work that brings the harvest.
The **kinara** (kee-NAH-rah) is a seven-branched candleholder. The candles are lit during Kwanzaa.	**Zawadi** (zah-WAH-dee) are gifts given on the last day of Kwanzaa. Most zawadi are handmade.
The **mishumaa saba** (mee-SHOO-mah SAH-bah) are Kwanzaa candles. They are black, red, and green.	The **kikombe cha umoja** (kee-KOM-beh cha oo-MOH-jah) is a large cup. It is used once during Kwanzaa.
The **muhindi** (moo-HIN-dee) are ears of corn. They remind us of the importance of children.	

Note To The Teacher: Use the Kwanzaa principles with "The Principles Of Kwanzaa" on page 23 and the mobile patterns with "Seven Celebration Symbols" on page 23.

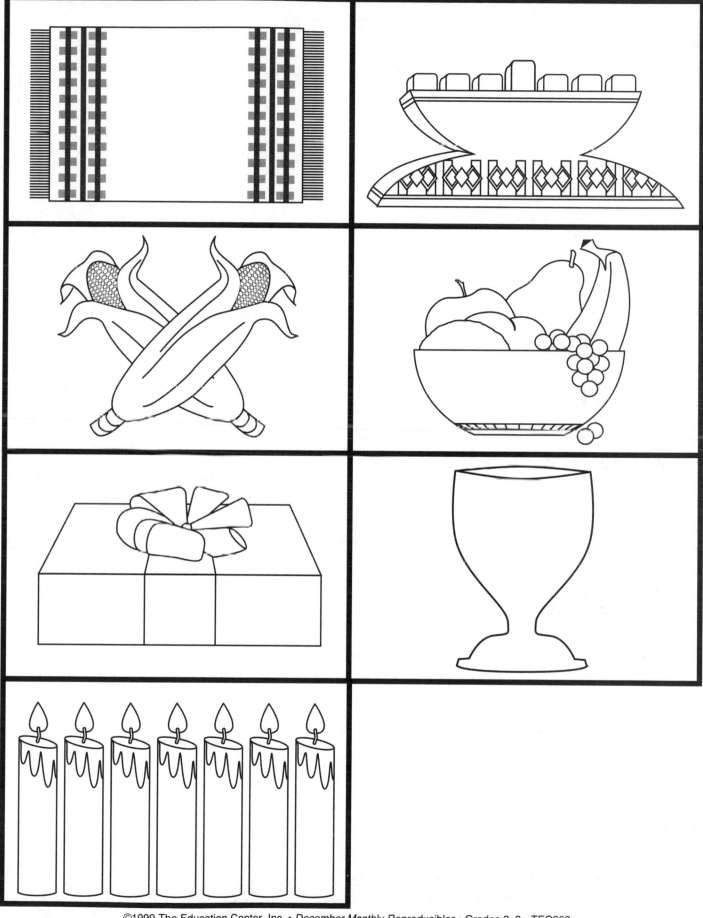

Note To The Teacher: Use with "Seven Celebration Symbols" on page 23.

Count On This Harvest!

Count by 2s, 3s, or 5s.
Write a numeral in each blank to complete the pattern.
Then color a fruit or vegetable to show the number
   pattern you used.

Kwanzaa means "first fruits of the harvest."

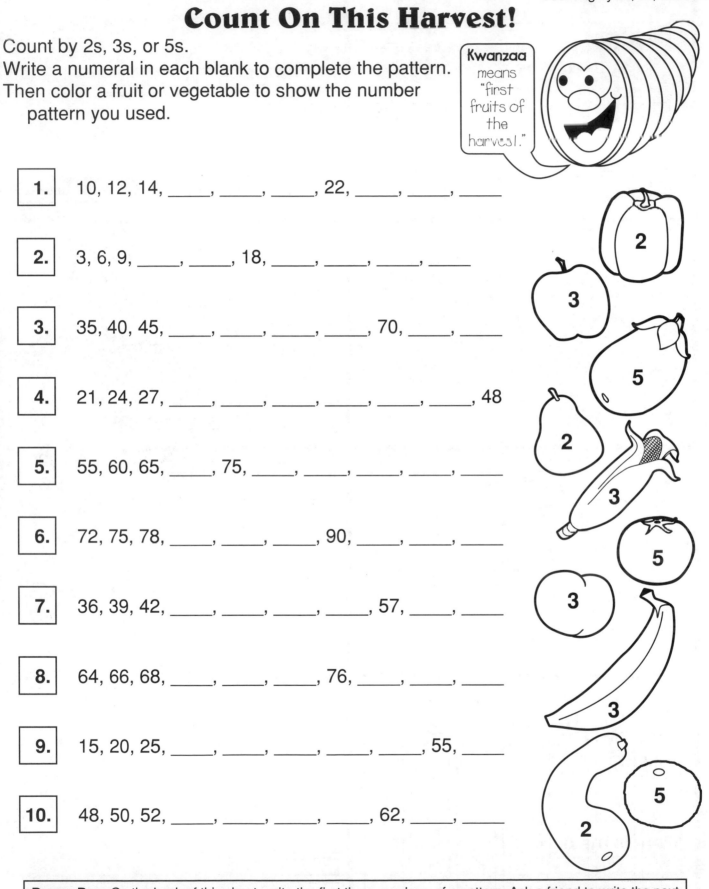

1. 10, 12, 14, _____, _____, _____, 22, _____, _____, _____

2. 3, 6, 9, _____, _____, 18, _____, _____, _____, _____

3. 35, 40, 45, _____, _____, _____, _____, 70, _____, _____

4. 21, 24, 27, _____, _____, _____, _____, _____, _____, 48

5. 55, 60, 65, _____, 75, _____, _____, _____, _____, _____

6. 72, 75, 78, _____, _____, _____, 90, _____, _____, _____

7. 36, 39, 42, _____, _____, _____, _____, 57, _____, _____

8. 64, 66, 68, _____, _____, _____, 76, _____, _____, _____

9. 15, 20, 25, _____, _____, _____, _____, _____, 55, _____

10. 48, 50, 52, _____, _____, _____, _____, 62, _____, _____

Bonus Box: On the back of this sheet, write the first three numbers of a pattern. Ask a friend to write the next three numbers in the pattern.

What's New?

It's a Kwanzaa custom to greet someone by saying, "What's new?"
To answer, the person says the principle of the day.

Find out the traditional way to say this greeting.
Solve each problem.
Then use the code to spell the greeting and the answer.

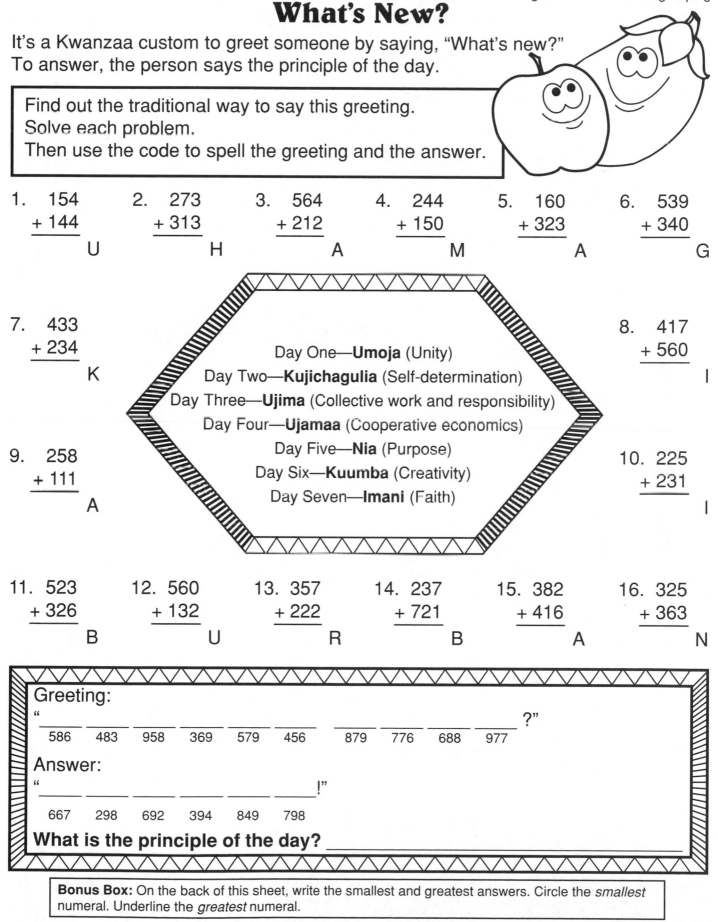

1. 154
  + 144
    U

2. 273
  + 313
    H

3. 564
  + 212
    A

4. 244
  + 150
    M

5. 160
  + 323
    A

6. 539
  + 340
    G

7. 433
  + 234
    K

8. 417
  + 560
    I

Day One—**Umoja** (Unity)
Day Two—**Kujichagulia** (Self-determination)
Day Three—**Ujima** (Collective work and responsibility)
Day Four—**Ujamaa** (Cooperative economics)
Day Five—**Nia** (Purpose)
Day Six—**Kuumba** (Creativity)
Day Seven—**Imani** (Faith)

9. 258
  + 111
    A

10. 225
  + 231
    I

11. 523
  + 326
    B

12. 560
  + 132
    U

13. 357
  + 222
    R

14. 237
  + 721
    B

15. 382
  + 416
    A

16. 325
  + 363
    N

Greeting:
" ____ ____ ____ ____ ____ ____ ____ ____ ____ ____ ?"
586   483   958   369   579   456   879   776   688   977

Answer:
" ____ ____ ____ ____ ____ ____ !"
667   298   692   394   849   798

What is the principle of the day? _____

Bonus Box: On the back of this sheet, write the smallest and greatest answers. Circle the *smallest* numeral. Underline the *greatest* numeral.

The Seven Days Of Kwanzaa

Kwanzaa is a seven-day holiday.
Each day has a special idea to think about.

Read the sentences.
Complete each boldfaced word with a suffix.
Color the candle as you use its suffix.
Then use four of the new words to write a paragraph about Kwanzaa.

1. The first day of Kwanzaa is for helping family and friends.
   It is a day for **together** _____.

2. The second day of Kwanzaa is about making decisions.
   We should not be **care** _____ when we make decisions.

3. The third day celebrates people working together.
   It is a day to be **help** _____.

4. On the fourth day we think about businesses in our neighborhood.
   We want neighborhood store owners to be **success** _____.

5. Day five reminds us to make our neighborhoods as great as they can be.
   We can work together for a **peace** _____ world.

6. The sixth day is a time for music, art, and dance.
   We show that our creative ideas are **end** _____.

7. The last day is for thinking about things we believe in.
   Many people are **thought** _____ on this day.

Bonus Box: On the back of this sheet, list three more words for each suffix:
-ful, -less, and -ness.

The candles are labeled: -ful, -ful, -ful, -ful, -less, -less, -ness

JAN BRETT

Travel is an inspiration to Jan Brett, so it's no surprise that her books take readers to faraway places. Prepare for a delightful literary journey as you explore with students this author-illustrator's books!

Flannelboard Favorite

Share with students one of Jan Brett's most popular books—her retelling of the Ukrainian folktale *The Mitten* (G. P. Putnam's Sons, 1996). In this humorous cumulative tale, a variety of animals, including a tiny hedgehog and a great bear, crawl into a mitten and make it their new home. After reviewing the story's events, have students create flannelboard characters to retell the story. Provide each student with a white construction-paper copy of page 30. Instruct him to color the patterns and cut them out. Next have the youngster glue a small felt square to the back of each pattern. (If desired, make several flannelboards. To make one, cover a sheet of cardboard with a large piece of felt and staple it in place.) Have pairs of students practice retelling the story with their characters on a flannelboard. Then arrange for each twosome to tell the story to one or two younger students. What a great way to boost retelling skills *and* develop cross-grade-level relationships!

The Story Within

Many of Jan Brett's beautifully detailed illustrations have borders that depict secondary story lines or hint at what will happen next. Show your students several examples of her artwork and discuss the stories within the borders. Then have each student design a picture story within a story. To begin, give each youngster a large sheet of drawing paper. Instruct her to measure on her paper a border that is about two inches wide. In the center of her paper, have her draw and color a picture of a special event in her life. Then ask each student to illustrate the details of the event in her border. Invite students to share their completed work, then staple it onto a brightly colored bulletin board titled "The Story Within."

Story Pop-Ups

Count on a love of books to pop up with this nifty project! Read several Jan Brett books with students (see "Sensational Stories" on this page for suggestions). Then give each student a white construction-paper copy of page 31. Instruct each youngster to summarize his favorite Jan Brett book on the writing lines, then color the border and background as desired. Next have him cut along the outside dotted line and fold his paper in half along the solid line. Instruct him to make cuts along the inside dotted lines as shown. Have him open his paper, pull the two resulting strips forward, and crease the tabs in the opposite direction from the fold. Instruct him to close the paper, press the folds, and then open the paper. Ask each student to create two construction-paper story characters and glue each one to the lower half of a tab. Then display the completed projects for all to enjoy!

My favorite Jan Brett book is "The Hat." Hedgie gets Lisa's stocking stuck on his head. All of the other animals think Hedgie looks funny. He tells them that he is wearing a hat. Then they wear some of Lisa's other clothes for hats. Hedgie thinks they look ridiculous! I do, too!

Sensational Stories By Jan Brett

Annie And The Wild Animals (Houghton Mifflin Company, 1990)
Berlioz The Bear (PaperStar, 1996)
The First Dog (Harcourt Brace & Company, 1992)
The Hat (G. P. Putnam's Sons, 1997)
The Wild Christmas Reindeer (PaperStar, 1998)

The Mitten Patterns
Use with "Flannelboard Favorite" on page 29.

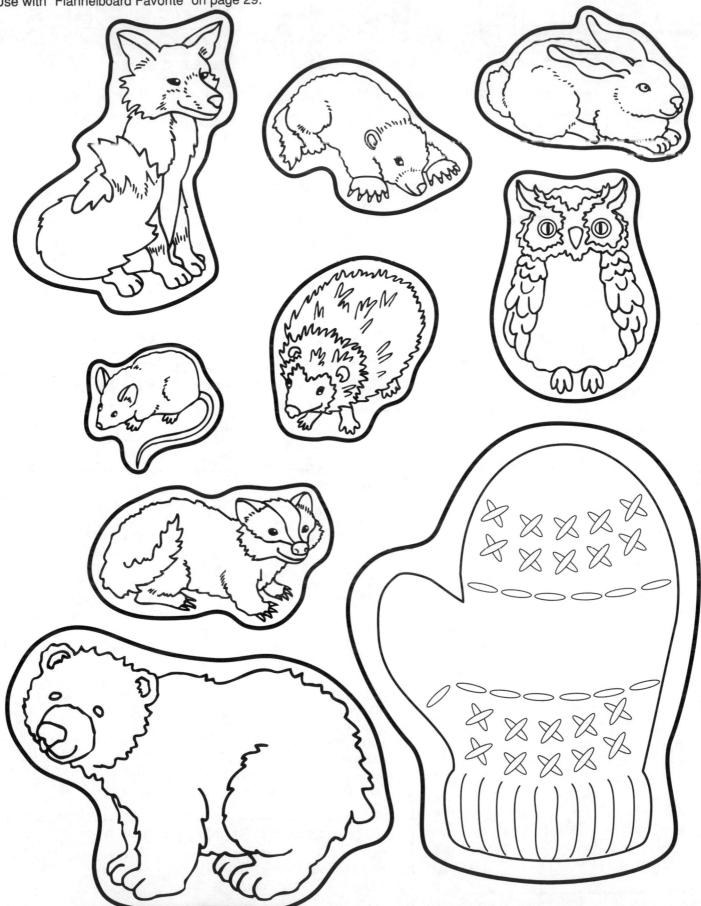

Fold.

Name _____

Jan Brett
Contractions

Treva And The Trolls

Read the sentences about *Trouble With Trolls*.
Underline each contraction.
Write the two words that make the contraction.

Treva decided that she shouldn't
take any chances. She carried Tuffi.   _____

Treva hasn't seen the trolls since she
skied away.   _____

Treva went up the path. That's where
the trouble began.   _____

Her feet wouldn't fit into the bindings.   _____

The troll grabbed the mittens.
Treva didn't notice that
Tuffi was missing.   _____

Think about the story.
Put the sentences in order.
Write the correct number on each hat.

Where does Jan Brett like to spend the
summers?
Unscramble the letters in the mittens to find
the answer.
Write the letters in the blanks.

u   i   o   n
n   t
a   s   m

the ___ ___ ___ ___ ___ ___ ___ ___ ___ ___

Note To The Teacher: Introduce this activity by reading with students *Trouble With Trolls* by Jan Brett (G. P. Putnam's Sons, 1992).

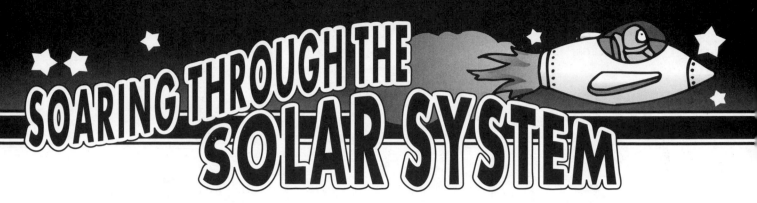

SOARING THROUGH THE SOLAR SYSTEM

Reach for the stars with this galaxy of ideas for studying the solar system!

Come To Order!

Prepare for takeoff with this lesson about planet order! Make a tagboard copy of each pattern on pages 34 and 35; then cut out the patterns. Laminate the cutouts for durability, if desired. Tape the Sun cutout to the center of a chalkboard or wall space. Explain to students that the Sun is the center of our solar system and each planet moves around the Sun in its own path, or *orbit*. Tell students about each planet in the order of increasing distance from the Sun (refer to "Planet Facts" on this page) as you tape it in place on the display. After reviewing the display with students several times, remove the cutouts. Program the back of each cutout with the ordinal number that corresponds with its planetary position; then place the cutouts in a center. To use the center, a student arranges the planets in order. Then he turns over the cutouts to check his work.

To extend the lesson, give each student a copy of the planet patterns (pages 34 and 35). Instruct him to color and cut out each planet, then glue it onto a separate sheet of drawing paper. Have him write the planet's name and a sentence about it. Next instruct the student to staple his pages in order between two construction-paper covers.

Planet Facts

The **Sun** is a star of average size and temperature. It is made of gases.

Mercury is covered with craters. Mercury looks a lot like our Moon.

Venus is almost as bright as the Moon at night. It has an orange-yellow sky.

Earth is the only planet with flowing water. About three-fourths of it is covered with water.

Mars is nicknamed the Red Planet. It has ice caps at its poles.

Jupiter is the largest planet. It has a red, stormy area.

Saturn is the second biggest planet. It has many rings made of ice, rocks, and dust.

Uranus is tilted so that it is lying on its side. It is blue-green.

Neptune is also blue-green. It is made of gases covered by ice.

Pluto is the smallest planet. It looks like a frozen snowball.

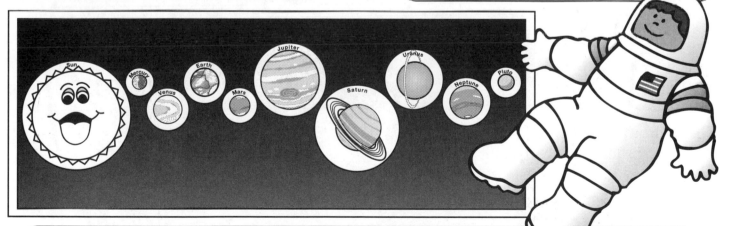

Solar System Snack

Has your study of the solar system inspired some future astronauts? Then give them more food for thought with this nifty activity! Explain to students that because there is no gravity in space, astronauts' food must be packaged in special containers. An astronaut often eats dehydrated foods sealed in airtight plastic bags. Once in space, he adds water to the food through a tube, then squeezes the food into his mouth.

To give your students a taste of eating in space, fill a class supply of small resealable plastic bags with applesauce or pudding. Give each student a prepared bag and instruct her to carefully snip off a small part of one corner. Then have her gently squeeze the food into her mouth while imagining that she is dining in space. Bon appétit!

Planet Patterns

Use with "Come To Order!" on page 33.

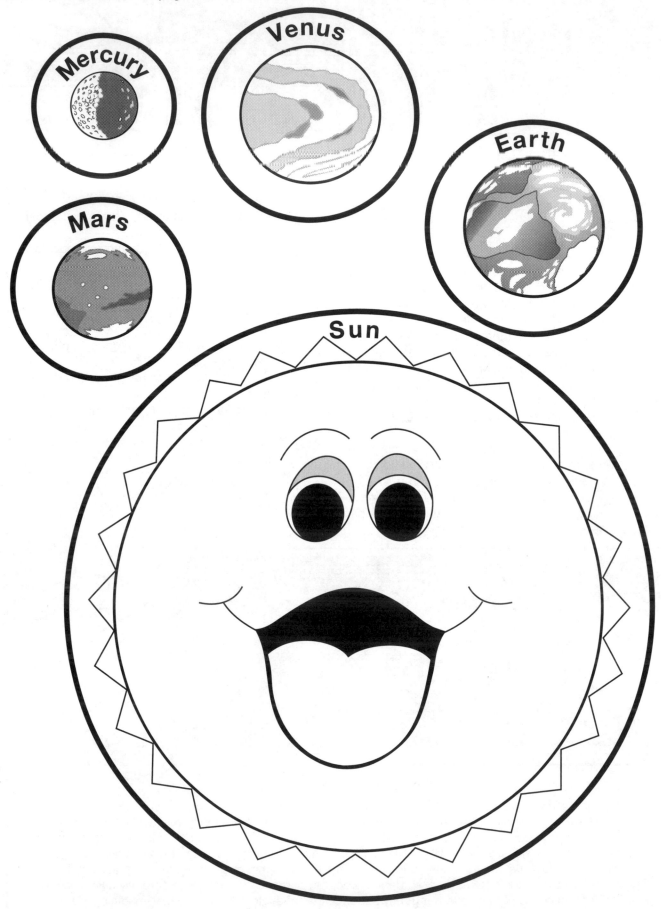

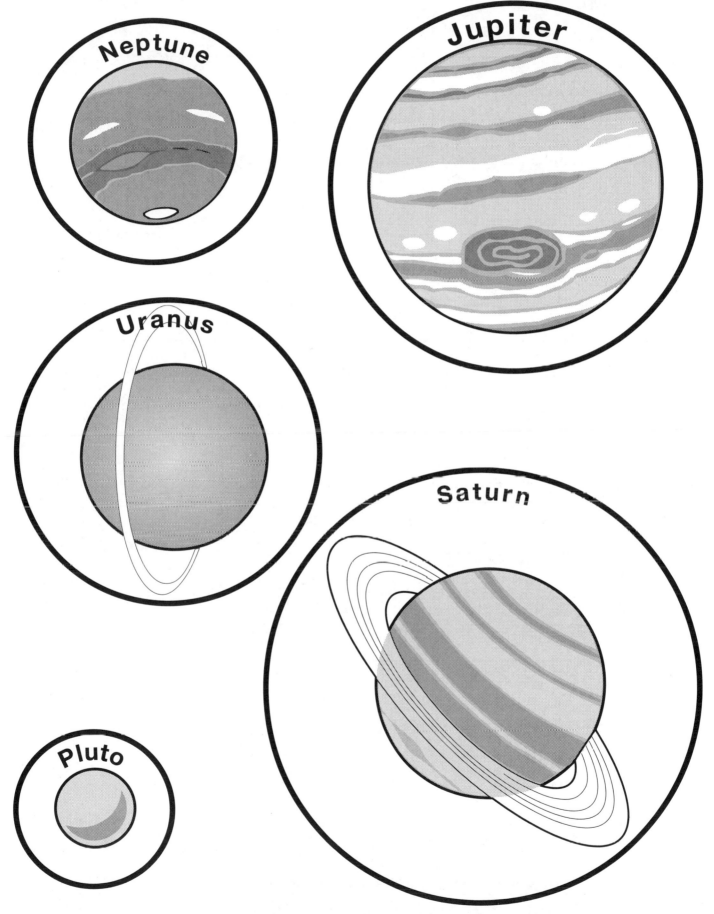

Name _____

My Journey Through The Solar System

Use the words below to write a story.

planet
asteroid
meteor
galaxy

rocket
Moon
comet
rotate

star
astronaut
satellite
orbit

gravity
Sun
universe
launch

Note To The Teacher: Discuss the words listed as needed. Then have each student use the words in a story. Define the topic and required story length, if desired.

36

Name _____

Mystery Place In Space

Use the clues and the Word Rocket to solve the puzzle.
Write each word in the matching puzzle row.
Find the name of the mystery place in the bold boxes.

1. All the planets orbit around the _____.

2. _____ is the smallest planet.

3. There are at least nine _____.

4. Our planet is called
_____.

5. _____ is known for its many rings.

6. _____ is the second
planet from the Sun.

7. _____ is the nearest
planet to the Sun.

8. _____ rotates
on its side.

9. The largest planet is
_____.

10. _____ is
made of gases and is
covered by ice.

11. _____ is sometimes called the Red Planet.

Word Rocket

Sun

Mercury   Saturn
Venus   Uranus
Earth   Neptune
Mars   Pluto
Jupiter   planets

What is the mystery place?

Note To The Teacher: Introduce this activity by sharing "Planet Facts" on page 33.

Name _____

Planets In Their Places

Read the sentences.

There are at least nine planets.
Each planet has its own place in the solar system.
Four planets are close to the Sun.
They are made of rocky materials.
These planets are called **inner planets.**

The five other planets are not as close to the Sun.
They are not as heavy.
They are called **outer planets.**

Draw a box around each inner planet.
Draw a circle around each outer planet.
Which object in the picture is not a planet? _____

Write the name of each planet on the correct list.

Inner Planets

1. _____
2. _____
3. _____
4. _____

Outer Planets

1. _____
2. _____
3. _____
4. _____
5. _____

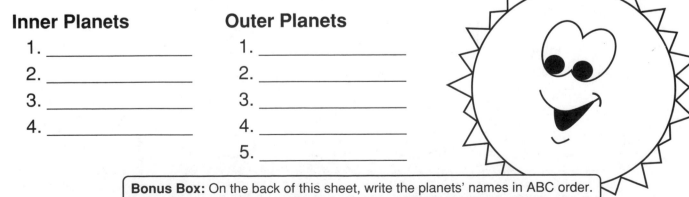

Bonus Box: On the back of this sheet, write the planets' names in ABC order.

38   ©1999 The Education Center, Inc. • *December Monthly Reproducibles* • Grades 2–3 • TEC969 • Key p. 64

Cosmic Calculations

Use a calculator to solve each problem. Write the answer on the planet at the end of the problem.

Remember, press **clear** before you start a new row!

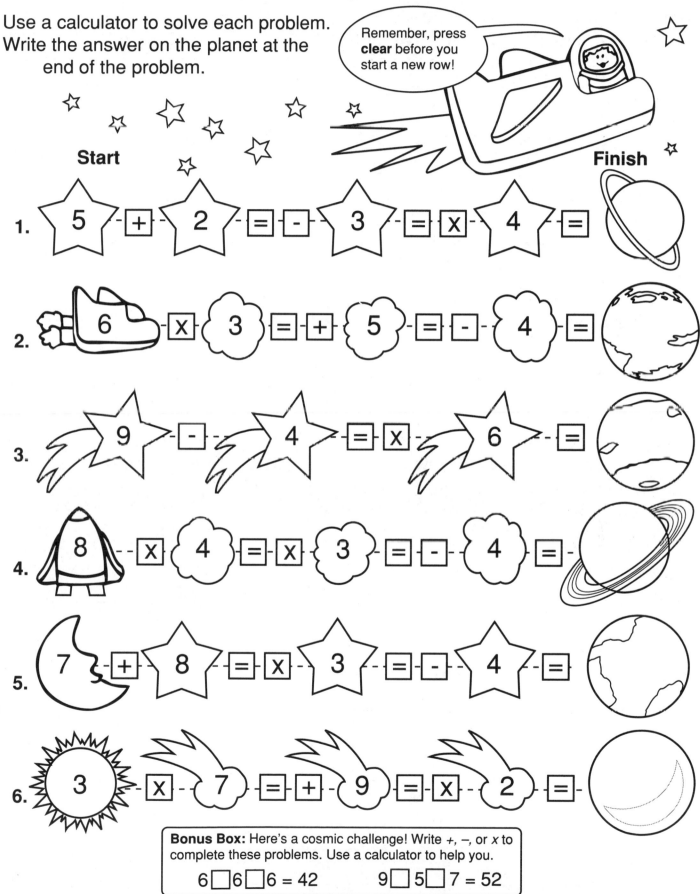

Start **Finish**

1. 5 + 2 = - 3 = x 4 =

2. 6 x 3 = + 5 = - 4 =

3. 9 - 4 = x 6 =

4. 8 x 4 = x 3 = - 4 =

5. 7 + 8 = x 3 = - 4 =

6. 3 x 7 = + 9 = x 2 =

Bonus Box: Here's a cosmic challenge! Write +, −, or x to complete these problems. Use a calculator to help you.

6 ☐ 6 ☐ 6 = 42   9 ☐ 5 ☐ 7 = 52

Martian Mail

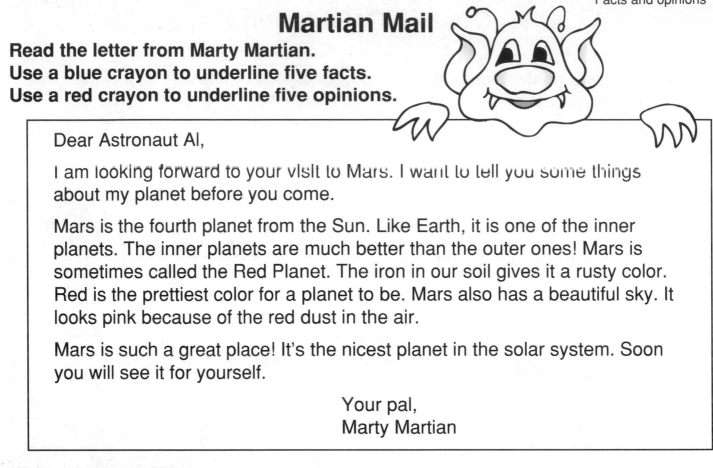

Read the letter from Marty Martian.
Use a blue crayon to underline five facts.
Use a red crayon to underline five opinions.

Dear Astronaut Al,

I am looking forward to your visit to Mars. I want to tell you some things about my planet before you come.

Mars is the fourth planet from the Sun. Like Earth, it is one of the inner planets. The inner planets are much better than the outer ones! Mars is sometimes called the Red Planet. The iron in our soil gives it a rusty color. Red is the prettiest color for a planet to be. Mars also has a beautiful sky. It looks pink because of the red dust in the air.

Mars is such a great place! It's the nicest planet in the solar system. Soon you will see it for yourself.

Your pal,
Marty Martian

Write a letter to Marty.
Include at least two facts and two opinions about Earth in your letter.
Use a blue crayon to underline each fact.
Use a red crayon to underline each opinion.

What do you get when you team up fun learning activities with one of the most popular stuffed toys? A terrific teddy bear unit guaranteed to please!

Guess My Bear!

Cute and cuddly, soft and snugly—teddy bears are a "paws-itively" perfect topic for descriptive writing! Ask each youngster to bring a teddy bear to school on a predetermined date. Be sure to have a few extras on hand for students who do not bring any. Have students brainstorm adjectives that describe their bears, and list their ideas on the chalkboard. Next ask each youngster to write a description of his bear on a sheet of writing paper, referring to the brainstormed list as he works. Collect the descriptions and bears. Then display the bears in a prominent classroom location. Randomly select a description and read it aloud. Challenge students to identify the bear described. Ask the student who wrote the description to verify youngsters' guesses. Continue in a similar manner until every bear has been matched with its description.

> **My Bear**
> by Charles
>
> My bear is brown. He has curly fur. He is wearing a blue and white striped hat. I named my bear Buttons because he has a vest with lots of buttons.

Teddy Bear Troubles

Sharpen students' problem-solving skills with this critical-thinking problem. Give each student a copy of page 46. Explain that the bears want to go outside to play, but their hats are mixed up. Tell students that it's their job to figure out which hat belongs to each bear. Read aloud the first clue. Lead students to conclude that the orange hat belongs to one of the girl bears. Have each youngster mark an X in the orange row under each boy bear's name to show that none of them has an orange hat. Instruct each student to read the remaining clues and mark each corresponding box with an X if the statement is not true for the matching bear. Then have him study his chart. Ask each youngster to add Xs where appropriate and to write "yes" in each box that shows a bear's hat color. Have him color the hats at the bottom of the sheet the corresponding colors. Then challenge each youngster to complete the Bonus Box activity.

Bear-To-Bear

This sweet center gives youngsters plenty of measurement practice with nonstandard units! Make a white construction-paper copy of the center patterns on pages 42 and 43. Color the patterns, cut them out, and laminate them for durability. Store the pieces in a decorated manila envelope. Place the envelope, a class supply of recording sheets (page 42), and a supply of Gummy Bears® candies at a center. To use the center, a student takes a card from the envelope. She lays Gummy Bears® candies, one beside another between the teddy bear symbols on the pictured object. Then she counts the candies and writes the number in the corresponding blank on the recording sheet. After the student has measured the remaining pictures, invite her to enjoy her candy for a delicious snack. Count on this center to be a sweet success!

Recording Sheet

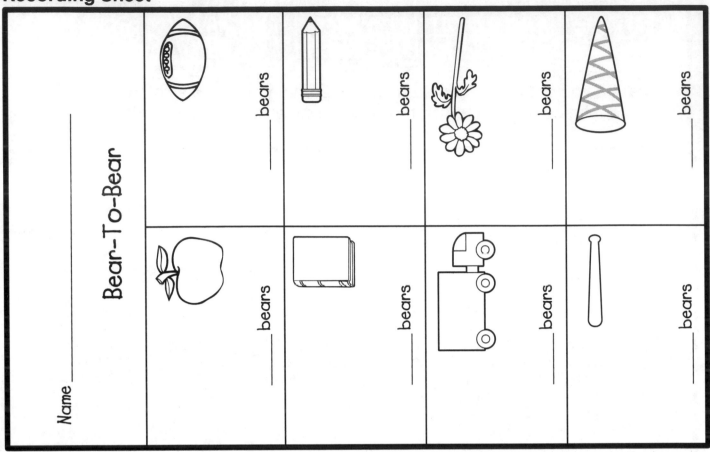

Bear-To-Bear

Name _____

_____ bears (football)
_____ bears (pencil)
_____ bears (flower)
_____ bears (tree)
_____ bears (apple)
_____ bears (book)
_____ bears (truck)
_____ bears (bat)

Center Patterns

Note To The Teacher: Use with "Bear-To-Bear" on page 41.

Note To The Teacher: Use with "Bear-To-Bear" on page 41.

Tina's Toy Mix-Up

Help Tina Teddy put her things in order.
Add *s*, *es*, or *ies* to each word in the toy chest.
Write the plural word below the matching shelf.
Draw a picture for each word on its shelf.

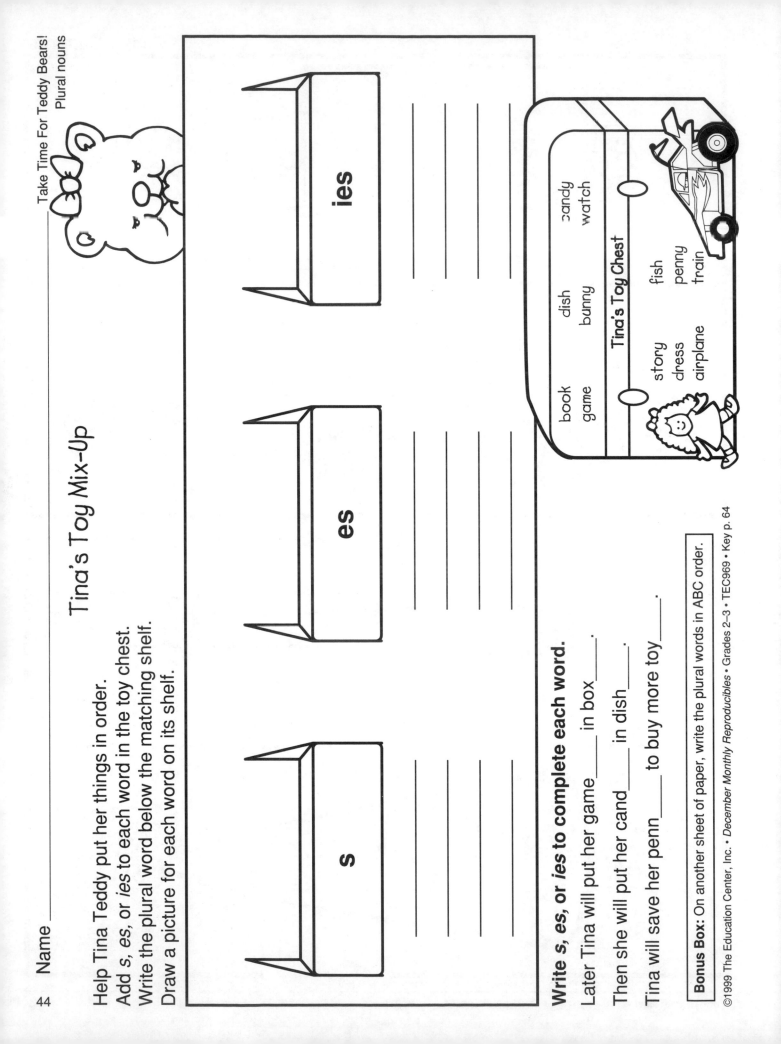

s

es

ies

Tina's Toy Chest

book   dish   candy
game   bunny   watch

story   fish
dress   penny
airplane   train

Write *s*, *es*, or *ies* to complete each word.

Later Tina will put her game_____ in box_____.

Then she will put her cand_____ in dish_____.

Tina will save her penn_____ to buy more toy_____.

Bonus Box: On another sheet of paper, write the plural words in ABC order.

Name _____

Teddy's Party

What is Teddy's favorite gift?
Look at each underlined digit.
Color its place value on the chart.
Then follow the path to Teddy's favorite gift.

	thousands	hundreds	tens	ones
1. 3,729	thousands	hundreds	tens	ones
2. 4,051	thousands	hundreds	tens	ones
3. 298	thousands	hundreds	tens	ones
4. 304	thousands	hundreds	tens	ones
5. 7,658	thousands	hundreds	tens	ones
6. 801	thousands	hundreds	tens	ones
7. 19	thousands	hundreds	tens	ones
8. 6,312	thousands	hundreds	tens	ones
9. 9,948	thousands	hundreds	tens	ones
10. 60	thousands	hundreds	tens	ones
11. 421	thousands	hundreds	tens	ones
12. 3,127	thousands	hundreds	tens	ones

Bonus Box: On the back of this sheet, write the greatest whole number possible with these four numerals: 6, 9, 1, 8. Then write the smallest whole number possible with the same numerals.

Teddy Bear Troubles

Help each bear find its hat.
Read the clues.
Use the chart to help you.
Color each bear's hat the correct color.
Then color the rest of the bears any colors you choose.

	Tom	Ted	Tina	Tony	Tracie
Red					
Blue					
Green					
Orange					
Yellow					

Clues

1. None of the boy bears wear an orange hat.
2. A boy bear has the blue hat. His name has three letters.
3. Tom wishes he had the green hat.
4. One bear's name rhymes with its hat color.
5. Tracie doesn't have an orange or a green hat.

Tom   Ted   Tina   Tony   Tracie

Bonus Box: After they play outside, the five bears will have cookies for a snack. There are 20 cookies. If the cookies are shared equally, how many cookies will each bear have? Show your work on the back of this sheet.

©1999 The Education Center, Inc. • *December Monthly Reproducibles* • Grades 2–3 • TEC969 • Key p. 64

This blizzard of activities and reproducibles is sure to cause an avalanche of learning fun!

One winter day I helped my neighbor shovel his driveway. We worked hard all morning! After we finished, we drank hot cocoa by the fire.

Cold Nose, Warm Heart

Brrr! Warm up to the topic of friendship with this heartwarming literature-based idea! Share with students a charming tale of friendship, *The Five-Dog Night* by Eileen Christelow (Clarion Books, 1993). In this wintry picture book, a grumpy man discovers that nothing can keep him as happy and warm as true friendship. Discuss how the man and his neighbor became friends; then ask each student to share one time that she helped someone. Next have each youngster write about her experience on a copy of page 48. Ask her to carefully color the dog pattern, leaving her writing visible. Then have her cut it out and glue it onto a sheet of construction paper. Bind students' completed work between two construction-paper covers titled "Cold Nose, Warm Heart!" No doubt students will love snuggling up with this class book on a wintry day!

Praiseworthy Snow Pal

Looking for a seasonal way to recognize positive behavior? Then try this snowy idea! In advance, cut several snowballs and a large snowman shape from white bulletin-board paper. Display the snowman cutout on an easily accessible bulletin board or wall. Then, from colored construction paper, cut a variety of features and accessories for the snowman, such as eyes, buttons, a nose, and a top hat. Duplicate a class set of the awards on page 49. Store the awards, snowballs, and snowman features and accessories in a basket or large manila envelope near the display. Each time a student exhibits positive behavior or achieves something that you would like to recognize, program an award and present it to him with a cutout. Help him mount the cutout onto the display in an appropriate place. When all the cutouts have been added, invite your youngsters to celebrate with a delicious snack of animal crackers and Rich Hot Cocoa (see the recipe on this page). Yum!

Rich Hot Cocoa

(Makes approximately 24 five-ounce servings)

You need:
3/4 gallon chocolate milk
2 cups milk chocolate chips
2 cups miniature marshmallows
Crock-Pot®

Directions:
Heat the milk in the Crock-Pot® on low for approximately two hours, stirring occasionally (do not boil). Then add the chocolate chips and marshmallows to the milk. Stir until the chips and marshmallows are completely melted. Serve.

Writing Pattern

Use with "Cold Nose, Warm Heart" on page 47.

"Snow-body" Does It Better Than You!

Presented to

_____

for

_____

_____
teacher signature

_____
date

Hats Off To You!

Presented to

_____

for

_____

_____
teacher signature

_____
date

Name _____

Have A Ball!

Cut out each scarf. Read the word.
Glue each scarf onto the snowman with a **synonym**.
For each snowman, write two more **synonyms**.

Remember, **synonyms** have nearly the same meaning.

clever

fast

beautiful

enormous

cheerful

©1999 The Education Center, Inc. • *December Monthly Reproducibles* • Grades 2–3 • TEC969 • Key p. 64

rapid

brilliant

gigantic

lovely

joyful

The Bear Facts

Read each story.
Underline the main idea.
In each box, draw and color a picture that shows a different detail in the story.

1. Jason and Anna made tracks in the snow. Then they rode their sleds down the big hill. Afterward they drank hot cocoa by the fire and played a game. Jason and Anna did a lot of things on this snowy day.

2. Scott and Macey were making a snowman. First they rolled three snowballs. Then they stacked the snowballs on top of each other. They asked Mother for a scarf and a hat. Finally, they added a carrot nose and two button eyes.

3. There was a big snowstorm during the night. When Emily and Evan woke up, they went sledding. They pulled their shiny, red sled up to the top of a hill. Emily and Evan took turns riding the sled down the hill. They had a lot of fun.

Bonus Box: Choose one of the stories on this page. On the back of this sheet, write five more sentences to continue the story.

Name _____

Word Flurries

Look at the **guide words** that each snowperson is holding.
Decide which **entry words** belong with the guide words.
Write the words on the lines.
Six words will not be used.

Remember, **guide words** are the first and last words on a dictionary page.

Entry Words

snow	ice	mitten	sled
mend	flake	skate	white
winter	flag	warm	tunnel
view	igloo	show	tracks
fireplace	middle	silver	water

shovel   spruce

trip   where   falling   melt

Bonus Box: Six words were not used. Use the words to write a winter story on the back of this sheet.

52   ©1999 The Education Center, Inc. • *December Monthly Reproducibles* • Grades 2–3 • TEC969 • Key p. 64

Name _____

"Snow" Joke!

Solve each problem.

16 + 15 **C**	27 + 18 **T**	46 + 38 **O**	37 + 39 **B**	27 + 35 **A**
17 + 6 **I**	23 + 29 **F**	55 + 17 **W**	48 + 49 **U**	25 + 29 **S**
39 + 41 **R**	16 + 26 **K**	37 + 18 **L**	28 + 18 **E**	

Why do geese fly south for the winter?

Use the code to solve the riddle.

___ ___ ___ ___ ___ ___ ___   ___ ___   ___ ___
76 46 31 62 97 54 46   23 45   23 54

___ ___ ___   ___ ___ ___   ___ ___   ___ ___ ___ ___!
45 84 84   52 62 80   45 84   72 62 55 42

Bonus Box: If six geese fly south each day, how many geese will have flown south in five days? Solve this problem on the back of this sheet.

Name _____

Get The Picture!

Solve each problem.
Connect the dots in order from the *least* to the *greatest* answers.

> **What is black and white and red (read) all over?**
>
> a _____

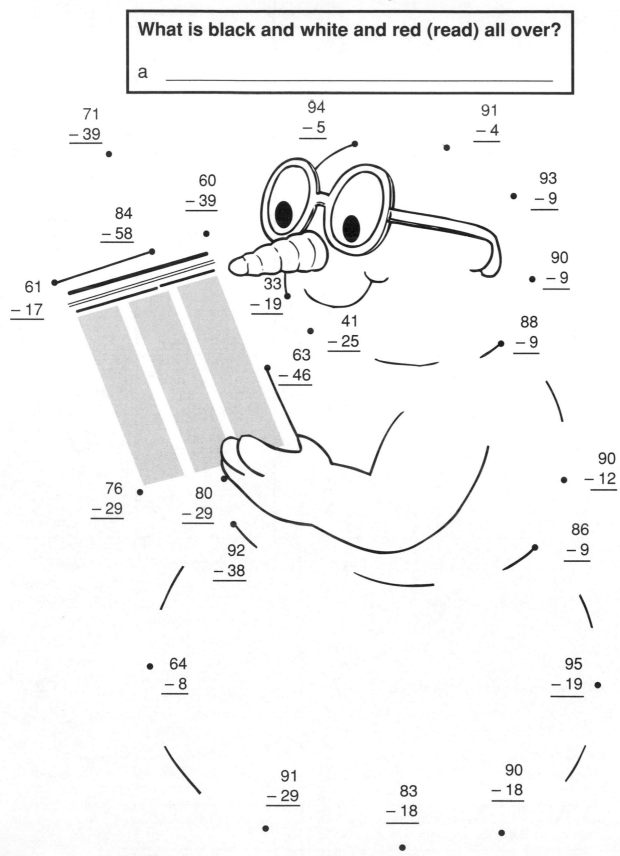

$$71 - 39$$

$$94 - 5$$

$$91 - 4$$

$$60 - 39$$

$$93 - 9$$

$$84 - 58$$

$$90 - 9$$

$$61 - 17$$

$$33 - 19$$

$$41 - 25$$

$$88 - 9$$

$$63 - 46$$

$$90 - 12$$

$$76 - 29$$

$$80 - 29$$

$$86 - 9$$

$$92 - 38$$

$$64 - 8$$

$$95 - 19$$

$$91 - 29$$

$$83 - 18$$

$$90 - 18$$

MITTENS, MITTENS, MITTENS!

These creative mitten activities are a perfect fit for your students!

Winter Reading Logs

Motivate students to read up a storm with these winter reading logs! In advance, gather a selection of books, including several books about mittens (see "Hands-Down Favorites" on this page for suggested titles). Have each student personalize and decorate a construction-paper folder for storing his reading log. If desired, instruct him to decorate it with the tracing technique described below in "Marvelous Mitten Art." Have each student personalize a copy of page 56. With each student's input, set a winter reading goal for him; then have him write his goal on the appropriate line of his log.

Throughout a designated period of time during the winter, ask each student to record on his log the books that he reads or has read to him. Provide additional copies of the reading log sheet as needed. Periodically celebrate students' wintertime reading accomplishments with a class treat, such as hot chocolate and cookies. For added wintertime fun, invite youngsters to tell their classmates about their favorite books as they enjoy their snacks.

Marvelous Mitten Art

Boost creativity with marvelous mitten art! Have each youngster draw a mitten on a 4" x 6" piece of tagboard and cut it out. Next, instruct him to make several overlapping tracings of his mitten at various angles on a large sheet of drawing paper. Then ask him to color each section of his resulting design so that no two adjoining sections are the same color. Have each student glue his project onto a slightly larger piece of colored construction paper. Display the projects on a wall or bulletin board titled "Marvelous Mitten Art."

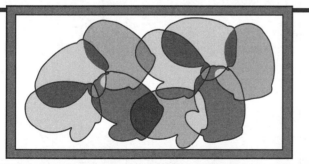

Hands-Down Favorites

The Mitten by Jan Brett (The Putnam Publishing Group, 1996)

The Mitten Tree by Candace Christiansen (Fulcrum Publishing, 1997)

Runaway Mittens by Jean Rogers (Greenwillow Books, 1988)

The Mitten by Alvin R. Tresselt (Mulberry Books, 1989)

Warm Up To Suffixes!

Pair up mittens and loads of learning fun with this suffix scavenger hunt! Tell students that a *suffix* is a syllable or syllables added to the end of a word to change its meaning. Give each student a colored construction-paper copy of page 57. Next, have her cut from discarded magazines and newspapers words with the suffixes shown. Have her glue each word onto her corresponding mitten. To complete the project, ask her to cut out her mittens and punch a hole at each dot. Instruct her to connect the mittens by tying an end of one yarn length through each hole. Collect the projects; then display them on a simple classroom clothesline or on a bulletin board titled "We're Warming Up To Suffixes!" Now that's a "hand-y" suffix reference!

____'s Winter Reading Log

Goal: _____

	Date	Title	Author(s)	It was read to me.	I read it with someone.	I read it alone.
1.						
2.						
3.						
4.						
5.						
6.						
7.						
8.						
9.						
10.						

My favorite book on this list is _____

because _____

Note To The Teacher: Use with "Winter Reading Logs" on page 55.

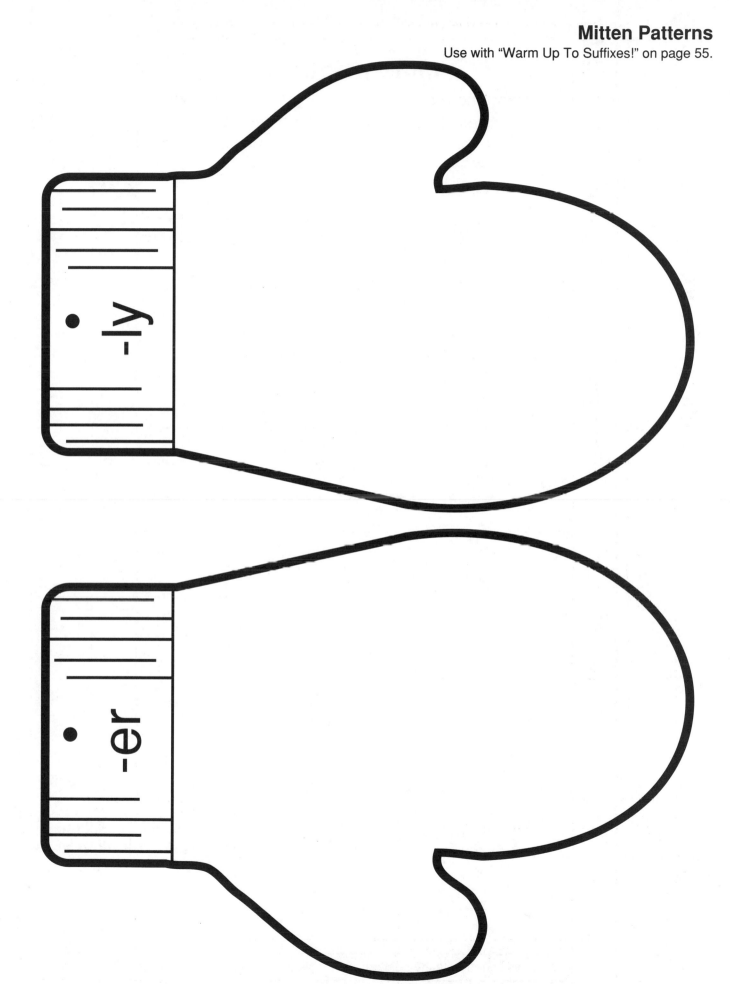

Name _____

Mitten Math

Use the code below to read the mittens.
For each pair of mittens, write a numeral that matches its code.
The first one has been done for you.

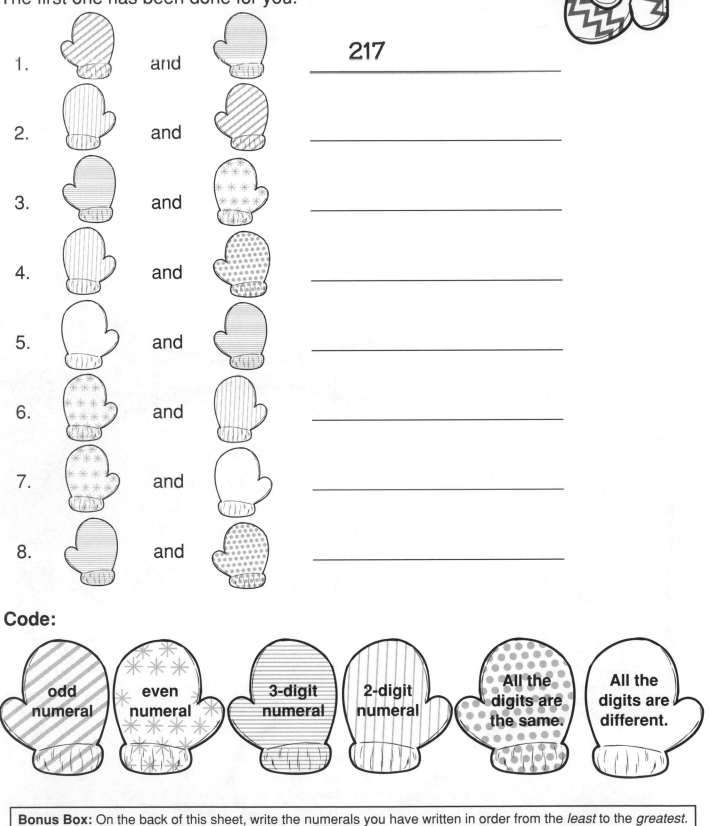

1. and   217
   _____

2. and
   _____

3. and
   _____

4. and
   _____

5. and
   _____

6. and
   _____

7. and
   _____

8. and
   _____

Code:

| odd numeral | even numeral | 3-digit numeral | 2-digit numeral | All the digits are the same. | All the digits are different. |

Bonus Box: On the back of this sheet, write the numerals you have written in order from the *least* to the *greatest*.

Poinsettia Day

Nothing says Christmas quite like a poinsettia! Honor this beautiful holiday plant and the man who brought it to the United States with this Poinsettia Day unit.

A Legendary Plant

Teach students about the history *and* the legend of the poinsettia with this unique booklet project! Show students a live poinsettia plant (or pictures of one if a plant is not available). Invite students to tell what they notice about the plant. Then share the facts shown on this page. Explain to youngsters that there are also *legends* (stories that have been handed down over many years, but haven't been proven true) about the poinsettia's origin. Read aloud *The Legend Of The Poinsettia* by Tomie dePaola (Paperstar, 1997). Then give each student a copy of page 60. Have her personalize her booklet cover and complete each sentence. Instruct each youngster to color her flowerpot and booklet cover. Next have her cut out the flowerpot and pages, then sequence her pages. Help her staple the pages to her flowerpot, then staple the flowerpot to a 4 1/2" x 12" piece of white construction paper (see the illustration). To finish her project, have her draw and color a poinsettia in her flowerpot. Encourage each student to share her completed legend booklet with her family.

Poinsettia Facts

- Poinsettia Day is December 12.
- The poinsettia was first brought to the United States from Central America by Joel Poinsett.
- More poinsettias are sold than all other flowering potted plants combined.
- A poinsettia's colorful leaves are called *bracts*.
- A poinsettia's leaves can be red, pink, white, yellow, cream, or peach.
- The poinsettia is also called *Christmas star, fire flower,* and *painted leaf*.
- Some poinsettias grow several feet tall.

Flowery Fact Families

Grow a garden of poinsettias with this fact-family activity! Give each student a yellow construction-paper flowerpot (if desired, duplicate the flowerpot pattern on page 60). Instruct him to write his name on the rim and draw a picture of his family on the pot. Then have him cut from colored construction paper two green and five large red poinsettia leaves, a green stem, and a yellow circle for a poinsettia center. Ask him to write the number of people in his family on the yellow circle. Then instruct him to write on each red leaf a number sentence with a sum or difference equal to the number he wrote. Next have him glue his poinsettia pieces together and glue his flower to his flowerpot as shown. Staple the completed projects to a bulletin board titled "Flowery Fact Families." If desired, add holiday decorations to give the display a festive touch.

Booklet Patterns

Use with "A Legendary Plant" on page 59.

The Legend Of The Poinsettia

by

_____

Padre Alvarez asks Lucida's mama to _____ a blanket.

1

Lucida and Mama buy _____ for the blanket.

2

A few days before _____, Mama gets sick.

3

Lucida tries to finish the _____, but she tangles the yarn.

4

Lucida becomes upset and _____.

5

An old woman tells Lucida that any gift is beautiful because it is _____.

6

Lucida places green _____ around the stable.

7

All the weeds in town turn into beautiful _____.

8

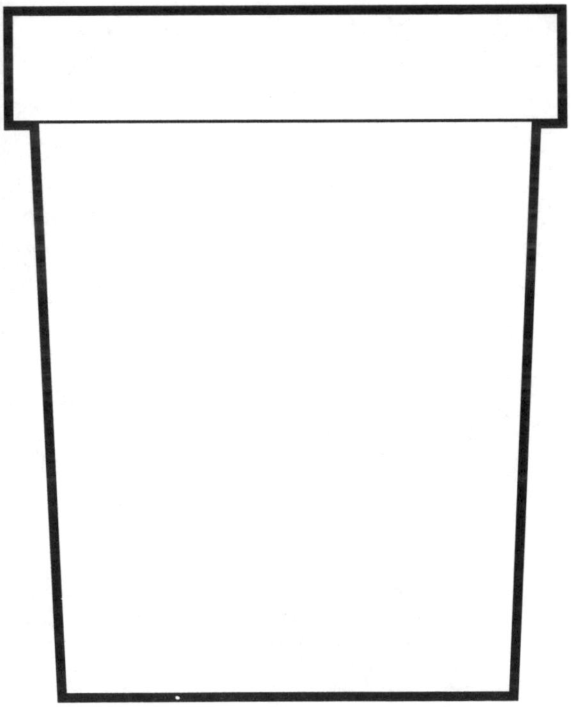

Pick A Poinsettia

Read the word on each flower.
Find the words in the Word Bank that have the same diphthong.
Write each word on a leaf of the matching flower.

flower

blew

oil

Word Bank

soil	chew	noise
flew	clown	town
frown	boil	point
how	coin	knew
threw	grew	owl

Bonus Box: On the back of this sheet, write two more words for each diphthong.

Plant Pot Pairs

Cut out each flowerpot.
Glue it above a rhyming word.

1. red	2. flower	3. leaf	4. stem

5. gift	6. bright	7. grow

8. petal	9. star	10. soil

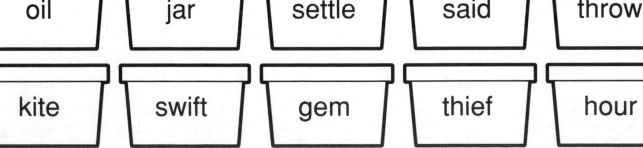

oil	jar	settle	said	throw
kite	swift	gem	thief	hour

Answer Keys

Page 8
1. 0 tens, 5 ones
2. 1 ten, 0 ones
3. 0 tens, 8 ones
4. 1 ten, 0 ones
5. 0 tens, 5 ones
6. 0 tens, 8 ones

Bonus Box: 38

Page 9
(The order of answers may vary.)

snowstorm
gumdrop
frostbite
gingerbread
toothpick
cupcake

Page 10
These gumdrops will be colored:
too
true
clue
blue
new
crew
stew
zoo
threw
to
who
blew
grew

Page 14
Before you start to cook, ask a grown-up to help you.

In a large bowl, mix together the potatoes, onion, and eggs. Add the flour, salt, pepper, and baking powder.

Carefully drop spoonfuls of the mixture into a skillet of hot oil. Flatten each spoonful with a spoon to make latkes.

Fry both sides of the latkes until they are browned.

Use a spatula to take the cooked latkes from the skillet. Place the latkes on paper towels to cool; then serve them.

Page 15
1. k
2. c
3. f
4. d
5. i
6. h
7. j
8. b
9. l
10. a
11. e
12. g

Page 20
1. 47 (green)
2. 66 (red)
3. 18 (red)
4. 99 (green)
5. 53 (green)
6. 14 (red)
7. 35 (green)
8. 76 (red)
9. 87 (green)

Page 21
1. **On M**onday the elves helped **S**anta read his letters.
2. **On T**uesday they decided what toys to make for **C**hristmas presents.
3. **W**ednesday morning was a very busy time at the **N**orth **P**ole.
4. **T**he elves were working hard to build toy trains for **S**anta's sack.
5. **T**hen an elf named **E**ddie spilled a can of red paint.
6. **H**is friends **E**llen and **E**rnie helped him clean it up.
7. **On T**hursday the elves helped **M**rs. **C**laus make dolls.
8. **A**ll day **F**riday, the elves wrapped candy for **C**hristmas stockings.
9. **B**y **S**aturday the elves were dreaming of vacations in **H**awaii.
10. **T**hey all agreed that **D**ecember is the busiest month of the year!

Page 22
1. baseball
2. boat
3. doll
4. drum
5. game
6. marbles
7. mittens
8. puppy
9. skates
10. sled
11. teddy bear
12. train

Page 26
1. 10, 12, 14, <u>16</u>, <u>18</u>, <u>20</u>, 22, <u>24</u>, <u>26</u>, <u>28</u>
2. 3, 6, 9, <u>12</u>, <u>15</u>, 18, <u>21</u>, <u>24</u>, <u>27</u>, <u>30</u>
3. 35, 40, 45, <u>50</u>, <u>55</u>, <u>60</u>, <u>65</u>, 70, <u>75</u>, <u>80</u>
4. 21, 24, 27, <u>30</u>, <u>33</u>, <u>36</u>, <u>39</u>, <u>42</u>, <u>45</u>, 48
5. 55, 60, 65, <u>70</u>, 75, <u>80</u>, <u>85</u>, <u>90</u>, <u>95</u>, <u>100</u>
6. 72, 75, 78, <u>81</u>, <u>84</u>, <u>87</u>, 90, <u>93</u>, <u>96</u>, <u>99</u>
7. 36, 39, 42, <u>45</u>, <u>48</u>, <u>51</u>, <u>54</u>, 57, <u>60</u>, 63
8. 64, 66, 68, <u>70</u>, <u>72</u>, <u>74</u>, 76, <u>78</u>, 80, 82
9. 15, 20, 25, <u>30</u>, <u>35</u>, <u>40</u>, <u>45</u>, <u>50</u>, 55, <u>60</u>
10. 48, 50, 52, <u>54</u>, <u>56</u>, <u>58</u>, 60, 62, <u>64</u>, <u>66</u>

Page 27
1. 298
2. 586
3. 776
4. 394
5. 483
6. 879
7. 667
8. 977
9. 369
10. 456
11. 849
12. 692
13. 579
14. 958
15. 798
16. 688

Greeting: "HABARI GANI?"
Answer: "KUUMBA!"

The principle of the day is creativity.

Bonus Box: 298, 977

Page 28
1. togetherness
2. careless
3. helpful
4. successful
5. peaceful
6. endless
7. thoughtful

Page 32
(The sentences should be numbered as shown.)
1. Treva went up the path. <u>That's</u> where the trouble began. <u>That is</u>
2. The troll grabbed the mittens. Treva <u>didn't</u> notice that Tuffi was missing. <u>did not</u>
3. Treva decided that she <u>shouldn't</u> take any chances. She carried Tuffi. <u>should not</u>
4. Her feet <u>wouldn't</u> fit into the bindings. <u>would not</u>
5. Treva <u>hasn't</u> seen the trolls since she skied away. <u>has not</u>

Where does Jan Brett like to spend the summers? the mountains

Answer Keys

Page 37
1. Sun
2. Pluto
3. planets
4. Earth
5. Saturn
6. Venus
7. Mercury
8. Uranus
9. Jupiter
10. Neptune
11. Mars

solar system

Page 38
Which object in the picture is not a planet? the Sun

(The order of answers may vary.)

Inner Planets	Outer Planets
1. Mercury	1. Jupiter
2. Venus	2. Saturn
3. Earth	3. Uranus
4. Mars	4. Neptune
	5. Pluto

Bonus Box: Earth, Jupiter, Mars, Mercury, Neptune, Pluto, Saturn, Uranus, Venus

Page 39
1. 16
2. 19
3. 30
4. 92
5. 41
6. 60

Bonus Box: $6 \boxtimes 6 \boxplus 6 = 42$, $9 \boxtimes 5 \boxplus 7 = 52$

Page 40
Sentences with facts:
Mars is the fourth planet from the Sun.
Like Earth, it is one of the inner planets.
Mars is sometimes called the Red Planet.
The iron in our soil gives it a rusty color.
It looks pink because of the red dust in the air.

Sentences with opinions:
The inner planets are much better than the outer ones!
Red is the prettiest color for a planet to be.
Mars also has a beautiful sky.
Mars is such a great place!
It's the nicest planet in the solar system.

Page 44
(The order of answers may vary.)

s	es	ies
books	dishes	candies
games	watches	bunnies
airplanes	dresses	stories
trains	fishes	pennies

Later Tina will put her games in boxes.
Then she will put her candies in dishes.
Tina will save her pennies to buy more toys.

Bonus Box: airplanes, books, bunnies, candies, dishes, dresses, fishes, games, pennies, stories, trains, watches

Page 45
Teddy's favorite gift is the train set.

Bonus Box: The greatest number is 9,861. The smallest number is 1,689.

Page 46
Ted has a red hat.
Tom has a blue hat.
Tony has a green hat.
Tina has an orange hat.
Tracie has a yellow hat.

Bonus Box: Each bear will get four cookies.

Page 50
The scarves and hats match as follows:

clever	fast	beautiful	enormous	cheerful
brilliant	rapid	lovely	gigantic	joyful

Page 52
(The order of words may vary.)

shovel—spruce	trip—where	falling—melt
snow	tunnel	flake
skate	view	flag
show	water	ice
silver	warm	fireplace
sled		igloo

Entry words that were not used: tracks, winter, mitten, middle, mend, white

Page 53

C: 31	I: 23	R: 80
T: 45	F: 52	K: 42
O: 84	W: 72	L: 55
B: 76	U: 97	E: 46
A: 62	S: 54	

BECAUSE IT IS TOO FAR TO WALK!

Bonus Box: 30 geese

Page 54
The dots should be connected in this order: 14, 16, 17, 21, 26, 32, 44, 47, 51, 54, 56, 62, 65, 72, 76, 77, 78, 79, 81, 84, 87, 89

What is black and white and red (read) all over?
a newspaper

Page 58
The numerals should match the following descriptions:
1. (already completed)
2. an odd, 2-digit numeral
3. an even, 3-digit numeral
4. a 2-digit numeral with digits that are the same
5. a 3-digit numeral with digits that are all different
6. an even, 2-digit numeral
7. an even numeral with digits that are all different
8. a 3-digit numeral with digits that are all the same

Bonus Box: Answers will vary.

Page 60
1. weave
2. wool
3. Christmas Eve
4. blanket
5. cries (or hides)
6. given
7. weeds
8. poinsettias

Page 61
(The order of answers may vary.)

flower	blew	oil
frown	flew	soil
clown	threw	coin
how	chew	boil
town	grew	noise
owl	knew	point

Page 62
1. said
2. hour
3. thief
4. gem
5. swift
6. kite
7. throw
8. settle
9. jar
10. oil